EGYPT

GIFT OF THE NILE

Designed by Louise Brody
Edited by Barbara Rosen

Library of Congress Cataloging-in-Publication Data
Rossi, Guido Alberto, 1949–
   Egypt: gift of the Nile: an aerial portrait / photographs by
Guido Alberto Rossi; text by Max Rodenbeck.
      p.   cm.
   Includes bibliographical references and index.
   ISBN 0–8109–3254–7
   1. Egypt — Description and travel — 1981– — Aerial.   2. Egypt —
Aerial photographs.   3. Egypt — Description and travel — 1981– —
Views.   I. Rodenbeck, Max, 1962–   II. Title.
DT47.R67   1992
916.2'0022'2 — dc20   91–27602
                                                              CIP

Copyright © 1991 Editions Didier Millet

Published in 1992 by Harry N. Abrams, Incorporated, New York
A Times Mirror Company

Printed and bound in Italy

EGYPT
GIFT OF THE NILE

AN AERIAL PORTRAIT

PHOTOGRAPHS BY GUIDO ALBERTO ROSSI   TEXT BY MAX RODENBECK

HARRY N. ABRAMS, INC., PUBLISHERS

CONTENTS

EGYPT OF THE MIND

15

THE MONUMENTS

29

THE METROPOLIS

69

THE NILE

105

THE DESERT

149

THE SEA

175

MAP

204

INDEX

206

FURTHER READING

207

Medieval minarets
peek out among
modern apartment
blocks on a hazy
afternoon in Cairo.
The aerial view shows
how the city has
breached the natural
obstacle of the
Mugattam Cliffs in
the background. The
Citadel of Saladdin sits
on an outcrop of the
cliffs. PAGES 6/7: The
monuments of Philae,
near Aswan, were
moved to a new island
after construction of the
High Dam threatened
to submerge the
original site. The
Temple of Isis in the
foreground was built
during the rule of
the Greek-speaking
Ptolemies. PAGES 8/9:
Feluccas, their lateen
sails furled, line the
shore at Aswan, while
camels await the arrival
of tourist passengers for
a jaunt in the desert.
Also waiting are the
souvenir vendors at this
ramshackle Nile-side
bazaar. PAGES 10/11:
These partly
reconstructed ruins
in the vast funerary
complex of Saqqara
just south of Cairo date
from the Old Kingdom
– about 2600 B.C.
Archeologists believe
they formed part of
a model of the
Pharaoh's palace.

EGYPT OF THE MIND

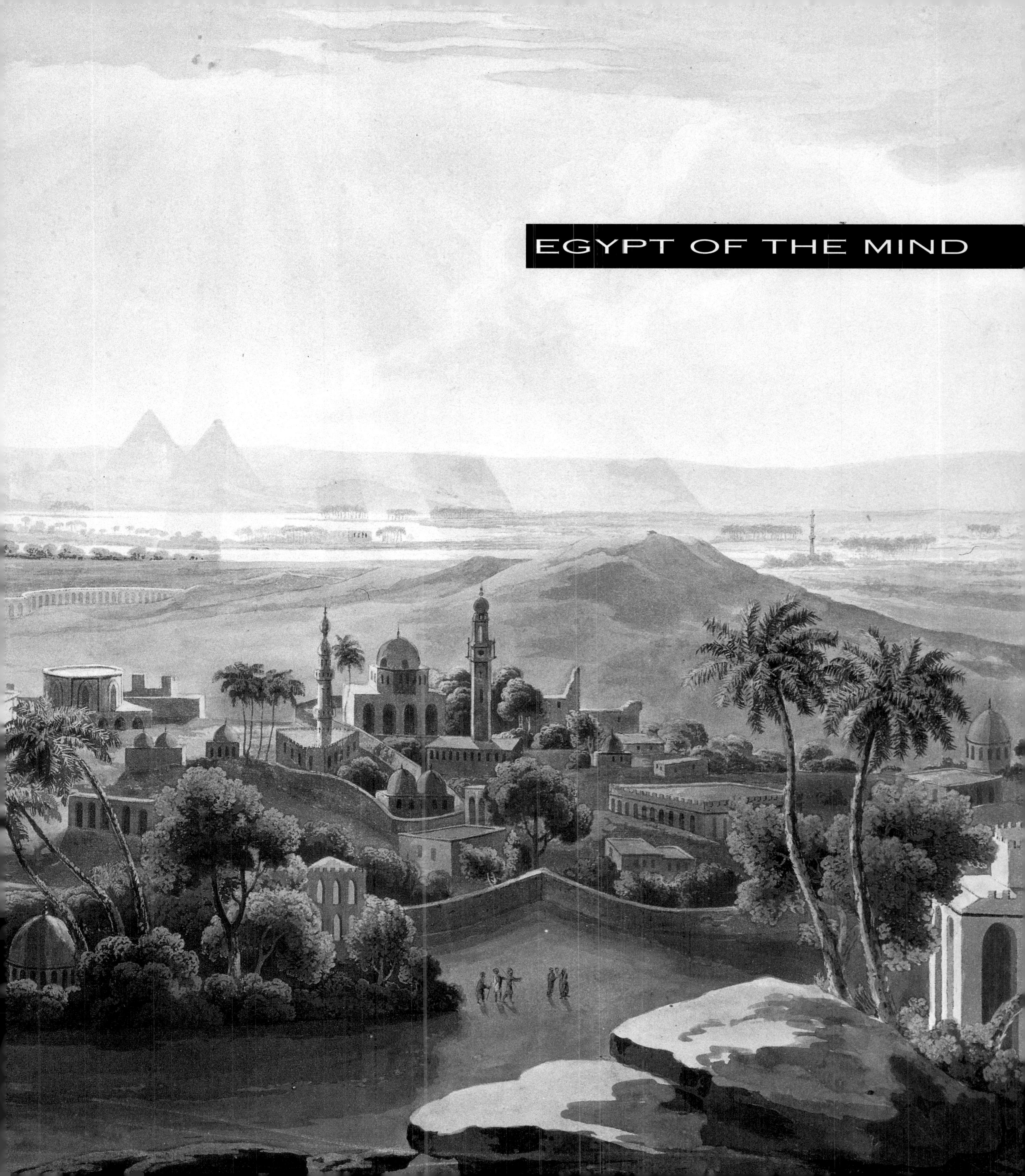

From above, the miracle of Egypt has a unique clarity. Descending into Cairo, one passes over miles of blank sand. Suddenly, unmistakably, pyramids loom up, so large that flight charts mark them as dangerous obstacles. Then one is over Egypt's dust-yellowed metropolis, split by the narrow sheen of the Nile. Improbably soon the plane touches down, already in the desert again. In the space of minutes one has jumped across a valley more densely crammed with people – with their creations and their history and their tribulations – than any other patch of ground in the world.

Few places are as alive in the collective imagination as Egypt. Any schoolchild in Kamchatka or Tierra del Fuego can tell of the Nile, of the rolling desert and of the dark-eyed ancient Egyptians who built the pyramids. Pressed further he or she could likely finish off the picture with a smattering of camels and palms and a touch of oriental intrigue. So unshakable are the preconceptions that one nineteenth-century traveler declared "the most beautiful portion" of the Egyptian scene "was that which was invisible – that which came thither with me from the North." William Makepeace Thackeray, who jokingly claimed the Great Pyramid for the English humor magazine *Punch* in 1844, glibly counseled the Egypt enthusiast not to trouble with crossing the seas: "Let him paint the skies very blue – the sands very yellow – the plains very flat and green – the dromedaries and palm trees very tall – the women very brown, some with veils, some with nose rings, some tattooed, and none with stays – and the picture is complete. You may shut your eyes and fancy yourself there. It is the pleasantest way, entre nous."

But such ruminations haven't kept the curious away. Being the very core of the known world, Egypt has been the inevitable starting point for anyone wishing to know the world. Greek adventurers, Roman dilettantes, Christian pilgrims, Arab geographers, European explorers – all these seekers of edification have preceded the modern tourist. Among foreigners, Egypt has become something of a synonym for all that is strange. The Old Testament – not the most objective of sources – immeasurably influenced attitudes with its descriptions of cruel, capricious Pharaoh and the decadent "fleshpots of Egypt." To the Hebrew authors of the Talmud the country was renowned for the potency of its magic, so much so that their term for superfluous action, akin to our "taking coals to Newcastle," was "taking magic into Egypt."

In the fifth century B.C., the great traveler Herodotus expanded on what was different about the valley of the Nile and its inhabitants: "Not only is the Egyptian climate peculiar to that country, and the Nile different in behavior from other rivers elsewhere, but the Egyptians themselves in their manners and customs seem to have reversed the ordinary practices of mankind. For instance...to ease themselves they go indoors, but eat out in the streets, on the theory that what is unseemly but necessary should be done in

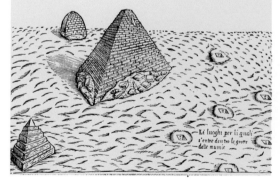

A seventeenth-century version of the pyramids. The holes in the ground purport to show where mummies are found: At the time, there was an extensive trade in "mummy powder," which was believed to be a cure-all. PRECEDING PAGES: A fanciful view of the Pyramids as seen from Cairo in 1809. The artist clearly recreated the scene from sketches: The Pyramids loom too large and pointy, the domes are too round, the minarets too square and the medieval aqueduct too long.

 1920s depiction of pyramid-building, complete with a cast of thousands, a massive wooden ramp and whip-wielding overseers. Still the pyramid is far steeper than any real-life Egyptian version.

private, and what is not unseemly should be done openly....In writing or calculating, instead of going, like the Greeks, from left to right, the Egyptians go from right to left – and obstinately maintain that theirs is the dexterous method....They are religious to excess, beyond any nation in the world ....They circumcise themselves for cleanliness' sake, preferring to be clean rather than comely...." And so on, with increasing consternation.

Nineteenth-century European visitors, imbued with their continent's newfound mix of objectivity and romanticism, reveled in the strangeness of their rediscovered Mediterranean neighbor. Sixty French savants accompanying Napoleon compiled the *Description de L'Egypte* – the first encyclopedic rendering of a single country. Edward Lane wrote his brilliant *Manners and Customs of the Modern Egyptians*, an early foray into cultural anthropology. Flaubert, like Napoleon before him, dolled himself up in what he considered oriental garb. The romantic poets feasted on Egyptian themes. In his "Ozymandias", Shelley (who in fact never saw the Nile) captured the image Europe imposed on Egypt: exotic, forbidding and decayed, but rich with residual wisdom.

To the amusement of Egyptians, their image of otherness has persisted through the ages, surviving successive revolutions that have utterly transformed the country's landscape, language, religion and way of life. Even the shrinking of the world – the expanded scale of modern tourism, growing sophistication about cultural diversity, increasing knowledge of history – seems to have left misconceptions about Egypt strangely intact. Indeed the unearthing of the country's pharaonic past by intrepid archeologists has added thickness to the stew, as have layers of virtue and fanaticism associated with the recent resurgence of Islam.

It may be that the Egypt of the Mind has fulfilled a certain craving, particularly acute in the rational and industrious West, for the more exalted, enduring qualities ascribed to Egypt. This may explain the recurrent fashion for things Egyptian like obelisks. Cleopatra's needles thus grace Istanbul, Paris, New York and London as well as Rome, which has no fewer than thirteen. Since the eighteenth century, smaller Egyptian-style monuments, with sphinx heads and outspread-wing motifs, have become standard in Western cemeteries. Egyptomania has influenced furniture and textile design, architecture, music and advertising. The nineteenth-century fad for Orientalist painting, replete with languid courtesans and fierce-looking Arabs, helped mold the West's imperialist outlook, especially among Europeans. And romantic Eastern imagery lasted into the age of cinema.

The weight of all this mental baggage leaves freshly arrived modern visitors frequently surprised – and sometimes disappointed – at what they find. Tourists have been heard to complain that Cairo, with its skyscrapers and underground Metro, is too modern for the city of *The Thousand and One Nights*. Yet in the same breath they are likely to bemoan the raucous metropolis' dirtiness: Hollywood never showed it that way. Likewise Arab visitors, drawn by a glittering entertainment industry, may feel let down

A contemporary painting shows how easily Napoleon's disciplined, well-equipped French forces overwhelmed the brave but outmoded cavalry of the Mamluks. Below, a seventeenth-century chart of Alexandria's Eastern Harbor reveals that by then, the great city had dwindled to little more than a fishing village.

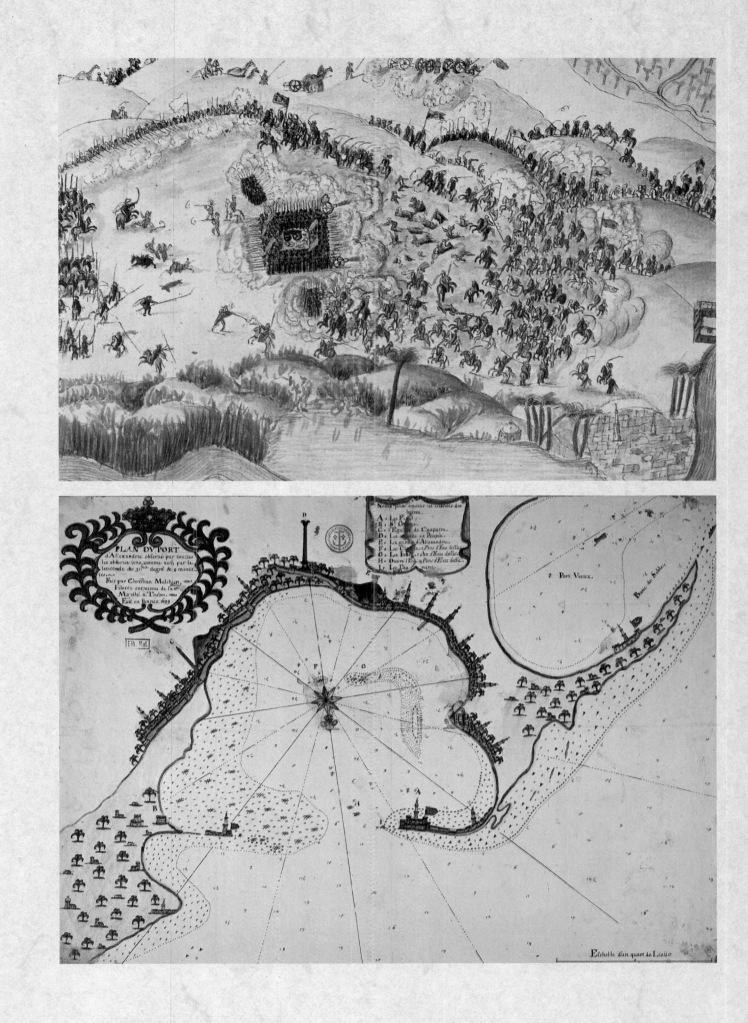

A massive head of Ramses II is hoisted out of reach of Lake Nasser, to the relocated temple of Abu Simbel. A campaign launched by UNESCO in the 1960s rescued Nubia's greatest monuments from the permanent flooding caused by the High Dam at Aswan. The Pharaoh's cheek is scarred with graffiti, but he looks otherwise unperturbed.

by the tawdry realities of Egyptian life. Asian and African Muslims attending Egypt's Islamic institutes are often shocked by the widespread private flouting of public piety. Particularly galling for some, the Egypt of the Mind is the ally of every trinket-hawker in the Valley of the Kings. These will gladly confirm their direct provenance from the noble Ramses, assure you of the magical powers of the Key of Life (a bargain at £50 a silver ounce) and swear to the antiquity of a rock from their neighbor's garden.

Yet these very surprises and regrets reveal that, unlike other tourist destinations, Egypt has resisted wholesale debasement into a theme park. True, if they wish to visitors can "experience" Ancient Egypt with a cruise to Dr. Ragab's Pharaonic Island near Cairo, where the skirt-clad staff act out scenes from an imagined past in front of plaster replicas of temples. They can chug down the Nile in motorized first-class luxury, or swish along in a lateen-rigged felucca. They can ride into the desert sunset on a feisty Arabian, or merely be hoisted onto a camel for the ritual pyramid Polaroid. All this is possible, but still there remains an Egypt which overwhelms the romantic gimmickry of the tourist trade. This is the place where Egyptians live, a place of which they are sometimes proud and sometimes ashamed. It is a place which, in seeking its way in an increasingly competitive world, carries the burden of an incomparably rich past. It is also a place every bit as fascinating as the imaginary one.

The Egypt of reality is a heavily urbanized country. A quarter of its people live in Cairo alone, jostling on public transport and working in offices and factories. They devour the crime and sports pages in the papers and addict themselves to TV serials. Like all players in the Middle East tragedy, they take a vocal interest in politics. In self-appraisal, Egyptians see themselves as the vanguard of Arabism and Islam, rarely as the last remnants of pharaonic civilization. Egypt has many of the sadder attributes of the Third World: illiteracy and malnutrition, gross disparities of wealth, corruption and abuse of power. Above all there is the intense pressure of overpopulation, which has swelled Egypt's cities and pushed its farmers beyond the natural boundary of the desert.

But if it is crowded and poor, modern Egypt also offers glimpses of timelessness — in rural and desert landscapes, in the kindness, cunning and fatalism of its people. Indeed it is the relaxed and world-weary Egyptians themselves who best preserve the spirit of their past. They may remain "excessively religious," but they temper the flaw with the stark realism of such folk wisdoms as: "The hand that you cannot bite, kiss." They may suffer from excessive pride, but counter it with a mercilessly self-deprecating humor. And the Nile is still the longest river in the world, its valley the most fertile. The unique contrast of desert adjoining rich farmland, of dead and vibrant civilizations side by side, is as dramatic as ever. Still, as Herodotus wrote, "More monuments which beggar description are to be found there than anywhere else." And meanwhile, the ancient African-Arab-Mediterranean-Islamic land transforms itself into something new and undiscovered. For a long time to come, Egypt will hold its spell on the world's imagination.

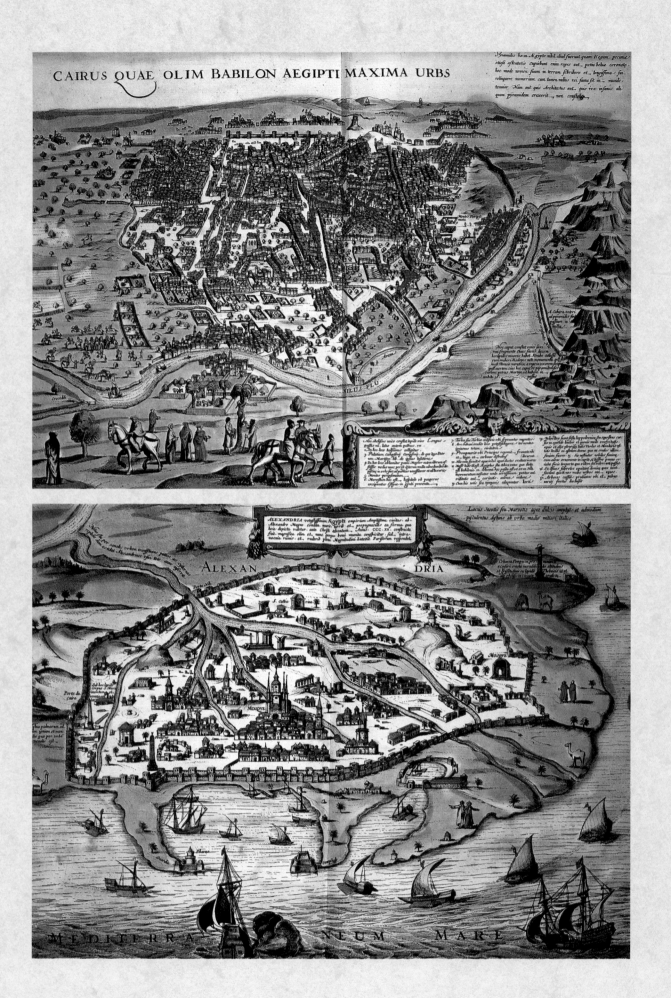

Above, Cairo as viewed in 1588. Accurately, the city is seen set back from the river on its eastern bank. Even some walls and streets are correct. But where is the Citadel, why are the Pyramids steeple-shaped, and why is the Sphinx facing the wrong direction? Below, Alexandria represented by the same artist. Again, some things are accurate, but a branch of the Nile is shown wrongly flowing through the city, and the two harbors are shown adjacent rather than back-to-back.

These two panoramas of Egypt were drawn by Hector Horeau in 1841. Above, we see the Nile Valley from the south, starting with the Temple of Abu Simbel, running through the monuments of Nubia and on to the Island of Philae at Aswan. In the distance are the ruins of Thebes and the Pyramids. Below is the same scene in reverse, with Alexandria at the bottom of the frame.

Above, a nineteenth-century lithograph shows feluccas at full sail. In the foreground scantily clad farmers raise irrigation water with a shadoof, still in use until recently. Below, a print by the English engraver David Roberts shows the Temple at Abu Simbel before the removal of its cozy cover of sand.

A favorite view of Cairo – from the Citadel, with the great madrasa of Sultan Hassan in the foreground. This one illustrated Henry Salt's 1809 volume on Egypt, where he acted as Britain's consul when not hunting for pharaonic treasures. Below, Roberts' 1840 view of Philae in its original state, before seasonal flooding caused by dams forced its removal to a higher island.

Above, a nineteenth-century recreation of the avenue of ram-headed sphinxes at Karnak, complete with Orientalist vegetable-sellers, cloth-merchants and fortune-tellers. Below, a sketch showing early steamships crossing the Suez Canal at Lake Timsah, where the modern city of Ismailia stands. Note the requisite picturesque natives in the foreground.

Above, a general view of the ruins of Karnak from a book by Belzoni, a famously rapacious early-nineteenth-century archeologist. Below, Roberts' exaggerated and spooky vision of the Temple of Edfu, which had not yet been excavated. Note the dwellings on the temple roof.

THE MONUMENTS

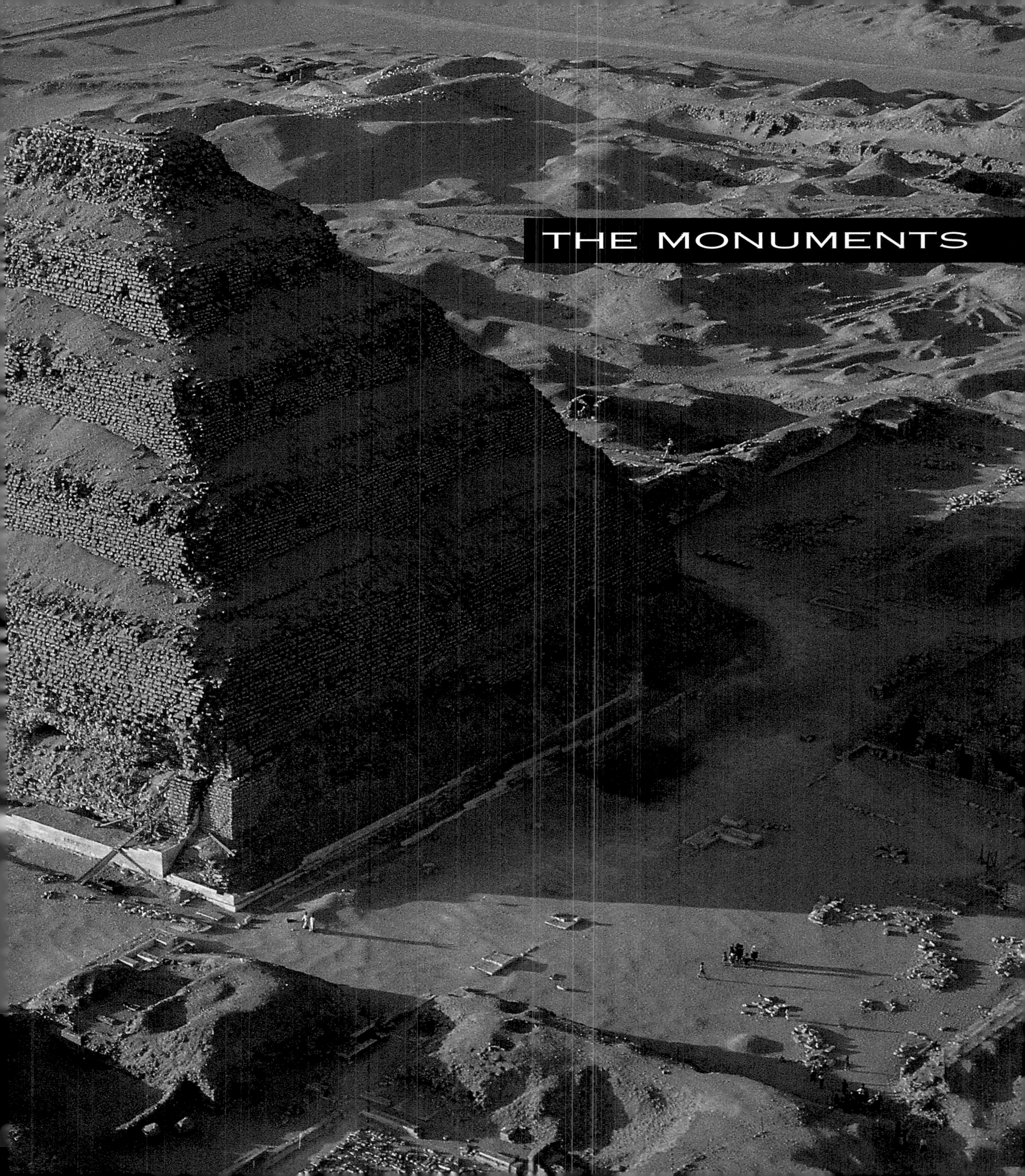

If there is a lesson to be learned from Egypt, it is about the passage of time. Always at the center of events and yet relatively secure from war and strife, the country is a register for both the past that is gone and the past that survives. Its history conceals no dark ages, no confusion of migrating tribes or shifting borders. Successive invaders — and there have been many — have seen their will eroded by Egypt's stubborn ways. The Egyptian scale neatly accordions man's 5,000-year stint of civilization into the stories of forty ruling dynasties — a manageable 200 generations. In this time the country has evolved from grand isolation under the Pharaohs — who make up more than half the dynasties past — to become first a Mediterranean power under the Greeks, then a rich but unruly Christian province under the Romans, and finally a bastion of Arabism under Islam. Providentially, Egypt's unparalleled wealth in monuments has preserved the legacy of each of these ages, with its religious beliefs and fashions and technologies.

The monuments of Egypt begin their tale many ages ago. The world's longest-surviving free-standing structure — the step pyramid at Saqqara — was built in about 2650 B.C. Three hundred years earlier, Egypt already had been unified under Mena, the founder of the First Dynasty and the first Pharaoh to wear the double crown of Upper and Lower Egypt.

Later ancients always looked back to the Old Kingdom, which ended with the fall of the Sixth Dynasty in about 2100 B.C., as a golden age. With a still-typical atavistic indulgence, the Egyptians considered its kings more just, its magicians more powerful. The reputation was well deserved: This earliest period in Egyptian civilization left the most exquisite of artworks as well as the mightiest of monuments. Its chiseled stone vessels were miracles of elegance, testifying to the Zen-like determination of their craftsmen. The tomb reliefs of Saqqara, with their brilliant and often amusing depictions of daily life, were seldom surpassed in inspiration or execution. Most impressive of all, the aesthetic ideals of the Old Kingdom endured with little change for two-and-a-half millennia: The standard proportions used in Egyptian sculpture were not revised until Roman times.

The pyramids, dozens of which poke out of the Western Desert near the ancient capital at Memphis, symbolize both the genius of their time and the power of the Old Kingdom Pharaohs. Those of Cheops, Chephren and Mycerinus at Giza are the best known — indeed they are arguably the most famous monuments in the world. But others, though less perfect in form, are equally awesome: the collapsed pyramid of Meidum, the rhomboidal pyramid of Dahshur, the elaborately inscribed pyramid of Unas.

The pyramids have inspired legend and theory in profusion. According to Greek travelers, in the fifth century B.C. locals already were spinning tales of the wickedness of the Pharaohs who enslaved thousands to build such gigantic conceits. In a sure sign of degeneracy, Cheops was

An avenue of ram-headed — or formerly ram-headed — sphinxes marks one of the approaches to Karnak near Luxor. A similar avenue three kilometers long once linked Karnak with Luxor Temple. PRECEDING PAGES: The Step Pyramid of Zoser at Saqqara is said to be the oldest standing structure in the world. It was a prototype for the later, smooth-faced pyramids.

This jumble of columns and roofs at Karnak gives an idea of the complexity of the site, where more than twenty temples and shrines cover an area of sixty acres. The enormous main temple is dedicated to the Sun God Amun. Added to by successive rulers beginning in 1500 B.C., the complex is an open-air history book — for those who can decipher its hundreds of thousands of inscriptions.

A long evening shadow emphasizes the geometric perfection of the Pyramid of Chephren at Giza. This is the second great pyramid – a corner of its bigger sister, Cheops, is visible at the upper left. Four football fields would fit easily into the area of Chephren's base. Part of the original smooth limestone facing survives, at the top of the structure. How elegant it must have looked when it was built in 2500 B.C.

said to have prostituted his daughter to pay for his monument. To Europeans in the Middle Ages the pyramids were the granaries of Joseph, where the wise prophet of the Bible stored seven years' worth of food. Cultists in recent times have posited that the pyramids could not possibly be mere tombs. According to some, they are gigantic water pumps. Others say they are radar for extraterrestrial communication.

Ancient Egypt owes its peculiar mystique largely to the fact that traces of the humble and mundane have vanished. What is best preserved are the trappings of priests and morticians. Our vision is colored by the exotic: the half-animal pantheon depicted on temple walls; the mummified hawks, baboons and cats; the elaborate rites of burial described in a vast liturgy that has outlived secular texts simply because it accompanied the quiet dead rather than the restless living.

Thus we know more of spells and incantations and curses than we do of contracts or poetry or criticism. It should be remembered, too, that it was not until the last century that sense again was made of hieroglyphics. For a millennium and a half the painstakingly drawn characters on papyri and tomb and temple walls were so much gobbledegook. Not until Champollion deciphered the Rosetta Stone in the 1820s were Orientalists constrained to control their imaginations.

Of the Seven Wonders of the Ancient World, only the Pyramids of Giza still stand. This is hardly surprising: They were built to last for the eternity of their occupants' afterlife. Similarly, what remains from the daily life of Ancient Egypt is not the houses of peasants or even those of nobles, which were made of friable mudbrick and reeds. Memphis now slumbers under palm groves. Ramshackle suburbs cover Heliopolis, where priests of the Sun God Ra once prospered. The great city of Tanis in the Delta is nothing but a vast and grubby mound of dirt.

What survived – aside from tombs – were the houses of the gods: the great Upper Egyptian temples of Karnak, Abydos, Luxor, Dendera, Edfu, Esna, Kom Ombo and Philae. Built by a painstaking technique of piling up earth into ramps, pushing stone blocks up the ramps and then removing the earth, these vast edifices must have awed the ancients as much as they do the modern tourist. Fronted by gold-tipped obelisks and huge banners, their brightly painted but dimly lit interiors filled with incense and scurrying, bald-headed attendants to the god, the temples were a focus of temporal as well as heavenly power. Initiates would periodically seek guidance from the image of the godhead. Apparently the ancients were satisfied when the bearers who carried the god's statue from its private quarters bobbed up and down to indicate a nod, or otherwise.

The priesthood of the later pharaonic age amassed enormous landholdings and vied with the kings in wealth and influence. Small wonder that much of the literature excavated from this time exhorts students to follow the priestly profession. One such

Ancient Egyptians built Luxor Temple, but modern Chinese constructed the adjacent riverside park. Locals complained when the Chinese workers cremated a dead colleague. Surrounded by the world's most extraordinary monuments to the afterlife, Luxoris had not witnessed such "barbarity" in 5,000 years! The little feluccas are for hire; few sailors on the Nile these days can make a living without tourism.

document from the Nineteenth Dynasty, echoing the feelings of modern bureaucrats, warns an acolyte of the drudgery in every profession except that of the scribe: The soldier is beaten and eats dreadful food, the fisherman stinks and risks his life among crocodiles, and so on: "I am told thou dost forsake writing. Thou givest thyself up to pleasures; thou settest thy mind on work in the fields and turnest thy back on the God's words. Dost thou not think how it fareth with the farmer when the harvest is registered? The worm hath taken half the corn, the hippopotamus hath devoured half the rest. The mice abound in the field and the locust hath descended....And now the scribe landeth on the embankment and will register the harvest. The porters carry sticks....They say: 'Give corn.' 'There is none there.' [he replies] He is stretched out and beaten; he is bound and thrown into the canal....But the scribe, he directeth the work of all people. For him there are no taxes....Prithee, know that."

Temples also served to glorify rulers. Vain and spendthrift Ramses II erected colossal statues of himself at Abu Simbel, in Memphis and at his own mortuary temple, the Ramesseum in Luxor. He inscribed the walls of Karnak with propaganda claiming a heroic victory over the Hittites. (In fact, Ramses was routed.) With equal sangfroid Egypt's Greek and Roman rulers used religion to their advantage. The Ptolemies, the illustrious Greek dynasty that inherited Egypt from Alexander the Great, went to great lengths to fuse Greek and Egyptian beliefs in the carefully concocted cult of Serapis.

The sensitivity of these foreign rulers explains why some of the finest specimens of Egyptian architecture date from late antiquity. Up until the Emperor Constantine's conversion to Christianity in the fourth century A.D., the Greeks and Romans continued to patronize and embellish the temples of Philae, Kom Ombo, Edfu, Esna and Dendera. On their walls even Roman rulers are depicted in self-consciously Egyptian style.

Sadly, some of the most magnificent monuments of ancient times did not survive. Herodotus, who visited Egypt in the fifth century B.C., claimed that the Labyrinth, now a jumble of pits and mounds near the oasis of Al Fayum, exceeded the Pyramids in grandeur. The famous symbols of cosmopolitan Alexandria, the library and the Pharos, fell victim to economic decline, war and greed. The famous tomb of Alexander the Great, known as the Soma, drew generations of pilgrims to the city from

Dendera Temple, with its beautiful proportions, seen from the north-west. Carvings on the outer walls of temples usually carried a political message – an early form of propaganda.

throughout the Hellenic world. But even before Egypt's conquest by the Arabs in the sixth century, it had vanished.

Later inhabitants plundered defunct cities for building materials as well as treasure. Stones and columns from Heliopolis propped up the walls and mosques of Islamic Cairo. In their monotheistic zeal, early Christians defaced images of the old gods at Philae and elsewhere. (To be fair, they were neither the first nor the last to do so.) From Roman times onwards obelisks and artworks were hauled off to the parks and museums

Huge banners once graced the niches built into the sloping façade of the Temple of Medinet Habu. It was built by the twelfth-century B.C. Pharaoh Ramses III, during whose reign Egypt was threatened by successive invasions. In a design typical of Egyptian temples, successive pylons and courtyards follow a single axis.

of Europe. In the Middle Ages, belief in the healing properties of mummy powder led to the pillage of tombs. Many already had been stripped of valuables – a papyrus from 1120 B.C. charmingly details the exploits of a gang of grave robbers.

Luckily, the successors of pagan Egypt left legacies as great as their forebears'. Christianity thrived along the Nile despite fierce Roman persecution; its early fervor is reflected in the desert isolation of such monasteries as Saint Anthony's, Saint Paul's, Saint Catherine's and those of the Wadi al Natrun. With the coming of Islam a wholly different aesthetic evolved, finding expression in the magnificent mosques and palaces of the new capital – Cairo. Unlike other great cities of Islam – Baghdad, Damascus, Samarkand – Cairo was never vandalized by invaders. This lucky fact has left it a veritable museum of medieval architecture, much of it from a time when the Muslim East was far more sophisticated than Europe. Still, Europe caught up. Its power in the modern age is reflected in the Beaux Arts, Deco and Bauhaus façades in Egyptian cities, in the stock exchanges and grand hotels of Cairo and Alexandria.

Since Egypt's 1952 revolution, change has been momentous. Cars, highrises, flyovers and factories clog the valley of the Nile. The High Dam at Aswan mutes the ancient annual rhythm of rising and receding flood. The sound of gasoline pumps has replaced the creak of the shadoof and waterwheel. No longer is the desert pristine and impenetrable.

Change has taken its toll on Egypt's monuments. All of Nubia now lies under the High Dam Lake. Only the greatest of its temples were saved by being hoisted above the water line during the 1960s. The dam has also caused a country-wide rise in the water table, which threatens to undermine the foundations of many historic buildings. Excavation itself has often proved unhealthy. Columns at Luxor Temple began to lean after an adjacent cache of statuary was unearthed in the 1980s. Tourism also brings hazards. Condensation from the breath of thousands of visitors has caused visible deterioration in tombs at the Valley of the Kings, prompting not a few archeologists to suggest that those and other sites simply be reburied. Even Cairo's medieval heritage is under threat from pollution, sewage and neglect.

But with all the transformation the modern world has brought, some things have never changed. Barren women still conduct fertility rites in Upper Egyptian temples. The country's rulers still boast of their victories and inscribe their names on every building. In the national psyche, even the ancient fascination with the afterlife has lingered. Despite official Islam's distaste for ostentation in death, the great nationalist leaders of the twentieth century – Saad Zaghloul, who won independence from Britain, Gamal Abdel Nasser, who overthrew the monarch, Anwar al Sadat, who led Egypt through war to peace with Israel – lie entombed in opulence, as if by Egyptian right.

As in ancient times, the temple at Esna stands in the middle of the town. The accretions of successive dwellers have raised the ground level around the building by ten meters. The stubbier minaret in the foreground is almost modern by comparison – but it was built seven centuries ago.

The Bent Pyramid at Dahshur is among the more unusual monuments. Egyptologists speculate that the change in its incline was made to speed construction when the Fourth-Dynasty Pharaoh Sneferu, its intended occupant, died suddenly. In support of this theory they note that the upper stories seem to have been built in haste.

The pyramids of Cheops, Chephren and Mycerinus at Giza dwarf the nearby modern constructions of Cairo. The larger two are as high as fifty-story buildings, and are built of five million tons of stone. After nearly 5,000 years, just how and why they were built remains a mystery. In the surrounding desert can be seen numerous smaller pyramids and tombs built for princes and nobles.

For centuries the
Sphinx at Giza, the
placid symbol of Egypt,
lay buried in the sand.
Now, the modern
plagues of air pollution
and rising groundwater
are proving more fatal
than time. From the air
its battered face looks
disproportionately
small; from the ground,
a trompe l'œil effect
makes it seem
bigger than it is.

A portion of the immense necropolis at Saqqara. Built adjacent to the ancient capital of Memphis, which lies in the valley just below the desert, Saqqara contains thousands of tombs. Many preserve exquisitely carved reliefs from the Old Kingdom. The Step Pyramid of Zoser and the adjacent court and buildings were the work of Imhotep, perhaps the first recorded architect in history. The causeway in the foreground leads to the stumpy Pyramid of Unas.

One of the earliest efforts at pyramid construction, the lone Pyramid of Meidum marked a stage between the building of stepped pyramids and that of smooth-faced ones. Its outer sheath collapsed sometime during the New Kingdom, exposing the three-stepped core. In its time, it would have been about half the size of the Pyramid of Cheops at Giza.

The seldom-visited Pyramid of Illahun at Al Fayum is the southernmost in the Pyramid Field that stretches through the Western Desert 100 kilometers north to Cairo. Its ruinous state is due to the fact that it was built of mudbrick. The immaculate fields nearby, contrasting with the desert, may better preserve a pristine look of pharaonic Egypt.

This small pavilion at the entrance to the Temple of Hathor at Dendera was devoted to fertility rituals. Although constructed during the Roman period, it is a well-preserved example of pharaonic style and technique in stone-working.

The beautifully preserved Temple of the Goddess Hathor at Dendera, which flourished from 400 B.C. into late antiquity. Among the carved figures under the lion-headed rain-spout are Cleopatra and her son by Julius Caesar, Caesarion. In the background, beyond ruins from the Roman and Christian periods, stand what remains of the temple compound's mudbrick walls.

The forbidding-looking Colossi of Memnon at Luxor are in fact harmless images of Amenhotep III. The mortuary temple they once guarded has all but vanished. Note the knee-high statues of the Pharaoh's mother and his wife. Greek and Roman tourists reported that the statues emitted a mournful wail at dawn, but this has not been heard recently. The Valley of the Kings, (right), enfolded by the desert cliffs west of Luxor, conceals the rock-cut tombs of Egypt's rulers in the New Kingdom. It was here that Tutankhamun's tomb, with its incredible trove of artifacts, was discovered in 1922. Most of the eighty-two other tombs here had been plundered long before, leaving only exquisite painted reliefs illustrating mortuary rites from the Book of the Dead.

Village houses crowd the site of Ramses II's mortuary temple near Luxor, known as the Ramesseum. Ramses the Great ruled for sixty years, sired eighty children and erected more monuments than any other Pharaoh. To the right, just beyond the stubs of a former colonnade, can be seen the giant feet of what was once a massive granite statue of the twelfth-century B.C. ruler. In the background are vaulted mudbrick chambers that served as temple storerooms. Above, ancient vandals beheaded these statues at the Ramesseum. But as is particularly evident from the air, the solidity of pharaonic building techniques made the temples themselves almost indestructible.

Wedged into the base of desert cliffs near Luxor, the temples of Deir al Bahari have a dramatic site. Above, the building at the left is the much-damaged mortuary temple of the Eleventh-Dynasty Pharaoh Mentuhotep I (circa 2000 B.C.) Next door is the grander temple of Queen Hatshepsut, one of the more colorful rulers of Ancient Egypt. It dates from 500 years later and boasts fascinating reliefs depicting a sea voyage to the Land of Punt – modern-day Somalia. At right, the starkly simple ramps and colonnaded terraces of Hatshepsut's temple show the massive pharaonic style used to brilliant effect. Wilful Queen Hatshepsut, one of only a handful of female Egyptian monarchs, usurped the throne at age 24. Throughout her thirty-four-year reign she defused chauvinist critics by wearing the Pharaohs' traditional false beard. Later rulers disapproved, and had her images in the temple defaced.

The temple at Karnak. The first court on the main axis was entered from the pylon on the left, outside of which can be seen an avenue of sphinxes. The small building at the back of the court housed three shrines that served as way-stations for ritual processions. In the foreground on the right is the roof of a temple added by Ramses III (circa 1175 B.C.) To its left is a modern storeroom housing shelves of artifacts. Obelisks were originally tipped in gold leaf to reflect the rays of the sun. This one (above), erected by Queen Hatshepsut, was bricked up by her successor Tutmosis III to obscure her memory. Note the faded color of the now-uncovered lower section. PRECEDING PAGES: Karnak is said to be the largest complex of religious buildings in the world, a sort of pharaonic Vatican City. The innermost sanctum, closest to us, is the oldest part of the Temple of Amun. The pylon in the distance dates from fifteen centuries later.

The central part of Karnak. Each of the higher columns on the upper left is twenty-two meters tall; they mark the main axis of the temple. Both of the obelisks visible just beyond originally had twins; the two pairs were separated by a pylon. A visitor in pharaonic times, walking in a straight line, would have traversed first a courtyard, then a giant colonnade, and then stepped between two obelisks and through a monumental portal to find himself between two even taller obelisks.

This bird's eye view of Luxor unravels the complexity of Luxor Temple, seen here from the innermost shrine looking toward the entrance. Note the obelisk beyond the outer pylon. Its twin was removed in 1833 and re-erected at the Place de la Concorde in Paris. The ribbed capitals of the nearest columns symbolized the bound reeds used to support simpler dwellings. Once a year, the ancients believed, the God Amun left his home at Karnak to visit Luxor Temple.

Begun by
Amenhotep III in
1400 B.C., the Temple
of Luxor was added to
by such illustrious rulers
as Tutankhamun,
Ramses II and
Alexander the Great.
Even medieval Islam
added a shrine, the
popular Mosque of
Abu al Haggag seen at
the upper right. In the
foreground scaffolding
props up a colonnade
threatened by rising
groundwater.

All that remains of the Temple of Khnum at Esna is the columned entrance hall. Although it was built during the Roman occupation it preserves a purely Egyptian style.

Inscriptions here record the affairs of Ptolemaic and Roman rulers up to the time of the Emperor Decius in the third century A.D. The capitals are in the form of lotus flowers.

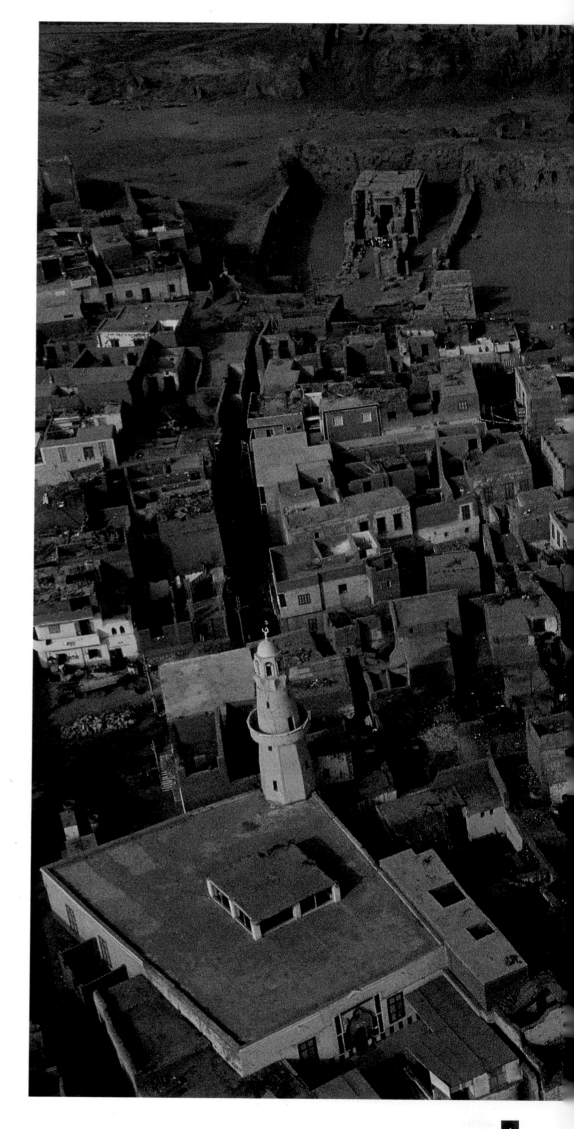

The Temple of Horus at Edfu was built over the short – for Ancient Egypt – period of 200 years, with the last touches added in 57 B.C. The elongated entrance pylon retains the same features as much-earlier gateways: the leaning walls, the figure of the Pharaoh raising his hand to strike down his enemies, the niches into which were fitted colossal flagpoles. Man-sized hawks carved from granite flank the doorway.

From the air one can see how astonishingly well preserved is the Temple at Edfu (right). One can easily imagine the arrival of the Goddess Hathor's great procession, which traveled upriver from her temple at Dendera once a year to reunite her with her husband Horus. The smaller, ruined structure to the left was a shrine for fertility rites. Note how the streets of the town still converge on the temple forecourt.

So popular was the Temple of Isis at Philae that it remained in use until the sixth century A.D., long after most Egyptians had converted to Christianity. After the building of the Low Dam at Aswan in 1902, visitors rowed through the half-submerged colonnades. The High Dam would have drowned it completely. Moving the temple to a new site was a mammoth undertaking, involving the careful dismantling and labeling of each individual stone. The elegant Kiosk of Trajan at Philae is known to locals as the Bed of the Pharaoh. Built under the Roman emperor of that name (circa A.D. 100), it served as a royal landing stage for the island temple.

The most grandiose of the Pharaohs, Ramses II, built the awesome statues of himself that guard the rock-cut Temple of Abu Simbel. The monument marked the limit of Egypt's domain, and was intended to convey the fearsome power of the Egyptian kings to visitors from the south. Twice a year the light of dawn penetrates to the deepest sanctum of the temple, illuminating an altar to the gods. Like Philae, Abu Simbel was moved to escape flooding from the newly dammed Nile. It now stands 200 meters above its original site and backs onto a hollow, artificial mountain. The smaller temple in the foreground (right) is associated with Ramses' favorite queen, Nefertari.

THE METROPOLIS

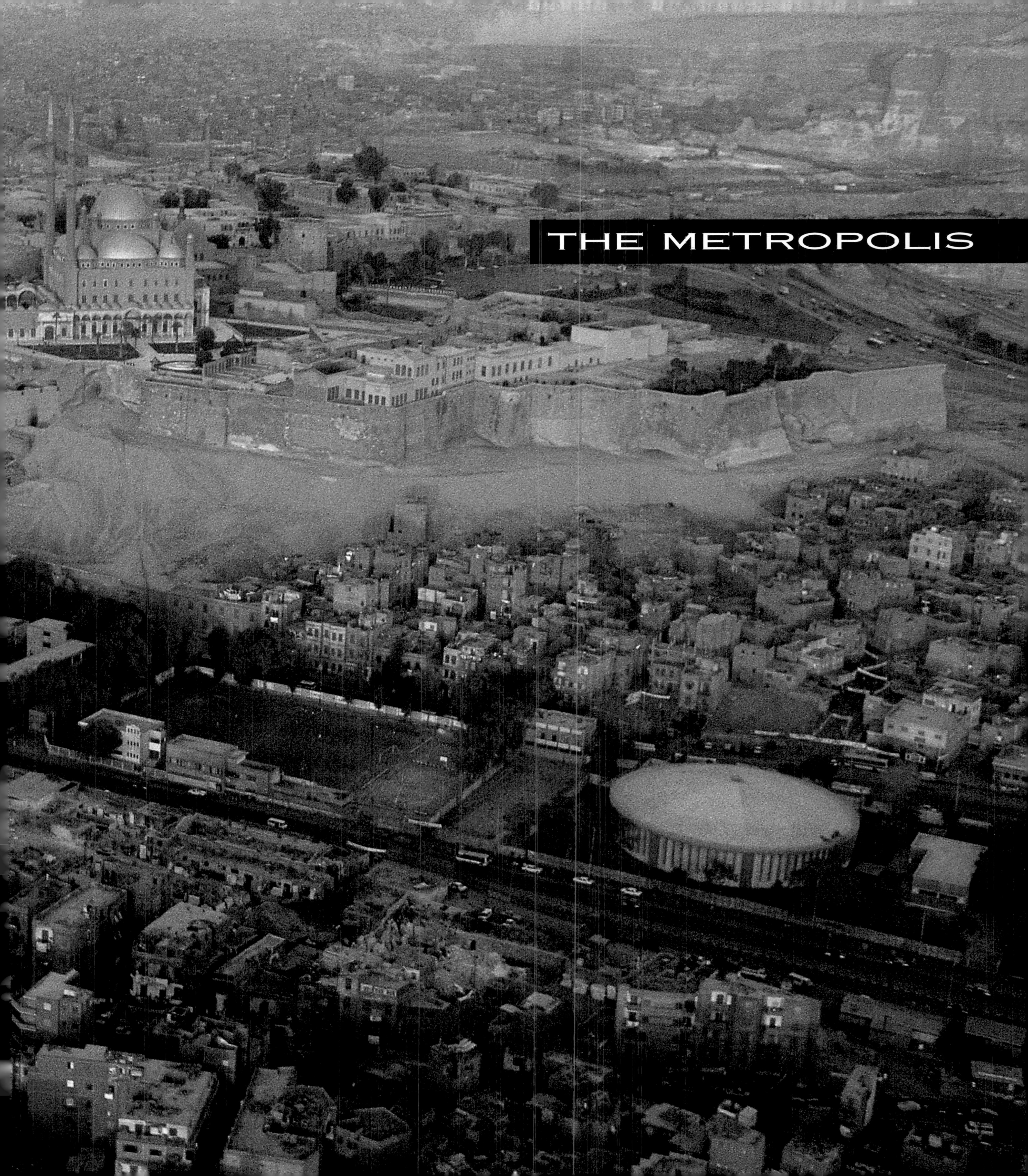

Not so long ago, the first that most visitors saw of Egypt was its flat, pale and dusty coastline. If they came by land, it was the soothing green of the Nile Valley which at last relieved days of dull desert ochre. Now all that has changed. Travelers fly direct to the country's heart, its showpiece, its despair. Without time for pause they succumb to the heaving, blaring traffic of Cairo. Soon its touts and beggars, its taxi sharks and perfume salesmen fight for their custom. Leering filmstars and neon squiggles of Arabic pulse at them from signboards. Egypt's great and tawdry capital assaults them with its smells: sweat and fenugreek, charcoal and rosewater, dust and incense.

Although the city has sprawled far beyond its medieval walls, and although the claxon and the loudspeaker have raised its decibels to new heights, the shock of arrival in Cairo has not changed so much since the time when caravans of spices, coffee or pilgrims on their way to Mecca plunged into the sudden darkness of its cramped streets. And in quite a few ways, life there has changed little since *The Thousand and One Nights* described its pleasures and intrigues. The stuff of wonder survives: tormented loves, timeless vendettas, piety, blasphemy, sophistication and squalor. Maybe this explains why the Arabic epithet for Cairo is Umm ad-Dunya or Mother of the World – meaning the world in the sense of worldliness.

But at perhaps 2,000 years of age Cairo, in Egyptian terms, is young. Its site was chosen for obvious reasons: at the head of the Delta for trade, at a narrowing of the river for easy crossing, at a point where the cliffs of the Eastern Desert close in on the valley for better defense. Strangely, however, there was no solid settlement here until Roman times, when a foreign colony flourished in what is now the Coptic quarter of Old Cairo. But in the Mediterranean empires of Rome and Byzantium, this outpost in the Egyptian interior held little interest. Its time for greatness awaited the arrival of a new invader.

Unlike the Europeans before them, the Muslim armies that conquered Egypt in A.D. 641 had no need of a Mediterranean capital. The rough desert Arabs preferred to encamp close to the routes back to Arabia, at a site from which they could easily control the Nile. The cosmopolitan Greek, Roman and Byzantine city of Alexandria declined, and Arab Cairo rose to take its place. By the fourteenth century, Cairo was probably the most populous city outside China. Over time, as the burgeoning city grew crowded and unruly, successive Muslim regimes built ever grander quarters for their courts and garrisons. In the ninth century, Ahmed Ibn Tulun, a Turkish emissary of the ruling Abbasid caliphs, prised the rich province of Egypt from its masters in Baghdad and built palaces, gardens, menageries and barracks to celebrate his independence. But his sons let the fiefdom decline. The Abbasid army that reconquered Egypt in 905 systematically demolished Ibn Tulun's constructions, sparing only his splendid mosque, of which the spiral minaret to this day evokes the ziggurats of Mesopotamia.

Cairo's impressive aqueduct was built by medieval Islamic rulers to carry Nile water to the Citadel. It runs for a distance of five kilometers. PRECEDING PAGES: Standing across the valley from the Pyramids, the massive Citadel of Saladdin housed the Muslim rulers of Egypt for more than six centuries.

The madrasa of Sultan Hassan, seen in the foreground, is one of the greatest monuments in Islam. Completed in 1356, it provided free lodging and training in Islamic law to 500 students. Its builder, a Mamluk sultan, lies entombed in splendor beneath the dome. The mosque of Rifai just beyond was built more than 500 years later. It is there that the last King of Egypt, Farouk, – and the last Shah of Iran, Reza Pahlavi – are buried.

Once, this part of the Imbaba quarter on the west bank of the Nile was a red-light district. The modern mosque here is popularly known as the Kit-Kat mosque after a now-defunct nightclub. Of the hundreds of house-boats that formerly moored along the Nile here, only a few dozen remain. All the buildings facing the Nile have been whitewashed as part of a government beautification campaign.

A half-century later the Abbasids lost their province for good. In 969 the Fatimids, an illustrious Shiite dynasty from North Africa, conquered Egypt and made it once again the centerpiece of an empire. To house their imperial court the Fatimids built another new quarter, naming it Al Qahira – The Victorious. Surrounded by the massive walls and gates that still enclose the older districts and adorned with mosques and palaces, Al Qahira was a magnet for scholars and mystics. The Fatimid caliphs, generous patrons, amassed a library of 100,000 volumes when Europe was at its lowest ebb.

Cairo – as European visitors pronounced it, extending the name for the new quarter to cover the whole city – had entered a golden age. For 500 years, under the Fatimids, then the family of Saladdin, and finally the slave dynasty of the Mamluks, the city was the capital of an empire that at its greatest stretched from Sicily to Armenia and southern Arabia. When one Fatimid caliph expressed a wish to taste cherries, which do not grow in Egypt, his attendants could produce a bowl the following day via the empire's efficient airmail: Informed overnight, a governor in Lebanon had hundreds of pigeons fly the fruit in relays to the capital.

With the decline of Andalusia in the west and the advance of Mongol hordes from the east, Cairo became a place of refuge for Muslim talent in every sphere. Craftsmen brought new influences and experimented with new styles. Workshops turned out pottery, glass, textiles and metalwork renowned for their fineness. Grown rich on the trade between Europe and the Orient, the wealthy vied in building the splendid mosques and palaces that make Cairo a showcase of Islamic art. The tenth-century college of Al Azhar, the Fatimid city walls of the eleventh century, the twelfth-century Citadel, the thirteenth-century tomb of Sultan Qalaun, the dozens of fabulous buildings from Cairo's peak in the fourteenth and fifteenth centuries – all survive to attest to the taste, wealth and craftsmanship of their builders.

The cost of land in the cramped urban environment inspired increasing sophistication in architecture. Buildings were designed to maximize interior space while showing off their dramatic features: grand portals carved and inlaid with colored marble, patterned domes that were miracles of geometry, minarets of ever-greater height and majesty. The architecture echoed the contrast between the utopian vision of Islam and the untidy bustle of crowded markets and alleyways. The mosque, with its clean courtyard and running water, its superb proportions and decorative patterns suggesting a geometric paradise, was the ideal antidote to surrounding disorder. Fountains and filtered light turned the houses of wealthy Cairenes into sanctuaries of repose.

Contemporary travelers exclaimed at Cairo's splendor. Nasir-e-Khusrau, a Persian gentleman of the eleventh century, wrote: "From a distant view the city appears as one lofty mountain bearing houses that compete with each other in height – one rising to seven stories, another fourteen....There are bazaars and streets perpetually lighted by tallow-burners, for the daylight

The Coptic Museum seen in the foreground stands on the site of a Roman fortress. In the background rises the circular Greek Orthodox Church of Saint George, built in 1919. The surrounding quarter is Cairo's oldest and is inhabited largely by Coptic Christians.

never penetrates and the place is a public passage." The wealthy and generous Fatimid rulers paid stipends to "a group of lords and princes from across the world," he wrote. "With no special occupation, they reside in court...wander around, greet each other, and retreat to their own quarters."

Three centuries later Ibn Khaldun, a Maghrebine diplomat, scholar and judge who retired to Cairo, wrote, "What one can imagine always surpasses what one sees, because of the scope of the imagination, except Cairo, because it surpasses anything one can imagine." The city was "the garden of the world, the anthill of the human species, the throne of royalty, a city embellished with castles and palaces, its horizon decorated with monasteries and with schools, and lighted by the moons and stars of erudition."

Emmanuel Piloti, a Venetian merchant who lived in Cairo during the fifteenth century, called it "the largest city that exists on earth, of those that we know...in the greatest prosperity of any city in the world." He went on to complain that because of Egypt's location, merchants had no choice but to cross it. This monopoly made the rulers in Cairo greedy – so greedy, in fact, with their taxes and duties that they drove adventurous Europeans to seek alternative routes to the Indies. Nor were the later sultans' exactions limited to trade. Powerful Mamluk beys with their own private armies dealt out summary justice to the populace, while rival factions clashed and rampaged in the streets.

Bad government was not medieval Cairo's only worry. The bubonic plague paid repeated devastating visits. So did famine. A twelfth-century traveler, Abdul Latif Baghdadi, described in convincing detail how Cairenes turned to cannibalism after a series of low Nile floods: Unwary pedestrians were caught on meathooks and hoisted into apartments. Mothers sold their children by the pound.

Time and again Cairo revived. But with its conquest by the Ottoman Turks in 1517, the city entered a long period of decline. The finest craftsmen were packed off to Istanbul. Portuguese ingenuity diverted trade around the Cape of Good Hope. Relegated again to the status of a province, Egypt became a backwater and a source of plunder. By the eighteenth century, large tracts of Cairo were uninhabited, the city surrounded by "dusty hills, formed by the accumulation of rubbish," according to Volney, a French visitor whose description was to inspire the curiosity of Bonaparte. As for the citizens, despaired Volney, "All that one sees and hears proclaims that one is in the land of slavery and tyranny."

Two churches stand side by side in the Coptic quarter of Old Cairo. The triangular roofing covers the naves. Much restored and altered, they were founded in the sixth and seventh centuries.

Into this sad city Napoleon's triumphant army marched in 1798, shocking Egypt into a new, competitive age. At first diplomatic, the French ended their stay by blasting cannon at captive Cairo. But it was French scientific achievements, not martial prowess, that impressed Egyptians most.

In the next century, under the dynasty founded by an Albanian renegade known as Muhammad Ali, Egypt struggled to find its place in the European-dominated order. Increasingly independent from Istanbul, its

The famous Cities of the Dead – vast cemeteries on the desert edges of Cairo – testify to the Egyptians' lingering concern with comfort in the afterlife.

rulers found a new source of revenue in cotton, which soared in value during the American Civil War, fueling Egyptian ambitions. The spendthrift khedives wanted all the trappings of the progressive nineteenth-century state: a rail network, a parliament, a civil code of law. But the great powers of the time grew wary of their competitors and worried by Egypt's mounting debt. In 1881 the British fleet bombarded Alexandria to "protect" European residents threatened by a rising tide of Egyptian nationalism. Soon after, the British army fought its way to Cairo, where it was to maintain barracks for more than half a century. Under the British protectorate Egyptian pride may have suffered, but the national purse did not. With the building of tramlines, museums and Parisian-style streets and villas, Cairo began to look less and less like the "oriental" city sought by European travelers. Windows and balconies replaced latticework screens and private courtyards. First the khedival court, then much of the Egyptian populace adopted western dress. In time, even cloistered womenfolk dropped their veils.

Alongside the old city, with its twisting alleys and fiercely independent neighborhoods, a planned municipality began to grow. By the turn of the century the two towns merged to form a polyglot whole of a million inhabitants. The complex medieval social fabric of tradesmen and pashas, Copts, Muslims and Sephardim was further complicated by the arrival of Greek grocers, Swiss businessmen, Italian craftsmen, Syrian traders and Middle European refugees. The two World Wars introduced another foreign element: Allied troops to whose urges Cairo catered with panache. But the high life led by the few, including King Farouk, who prowled nightclubs with his bodyguards, gave rise to resentment. In 1952 many of Cairo's European landmarks were burned by an anti-imperialist mob. The young army officers who soon took power oversaw a centralized, closely policed state, using the new medium of radio to inspire "the masses" with the spirit of nationalism.

In its republican age Cairo grew in stature. The Arab League made its headquarters in the wellspring of the new pan-Arab doctrine. Cairo's cinema industry cranked out slapstick and melodrama for audiences from Marrakesh to Muscat. Foreign-owned businesses were nationalized and the proceeds plowed into heavy industries. Once-leafy suburbs began to spew smoke. Expanded free education swelled the universities. The building of research institutes, cultural centers and row upon row of low-cost, highrise tenements reflected the newfound zeal for modernism at all costs. And Egypt's importance to the great powers of East and West was reflected in a Japanese opera house, a French Metro and dozens of other monuments to foreign aid.

As Cairo's inexorably expanding population surges beyond twelve million, as many as 150,000 people live in one square kilometer, crammed four and five to a room. A million cars clog the roads. Some schools work three shifts a day to cope with demand. And the fight for space, for money and for attention has left its mark on the Cairene character, once so patient and fatalistic.

Some half a million Cairenes live in the great tomb cities. With their wide streets and open courtyards, it is easy to see the attraction when compared to the noise and density of the rest of the city. In the far background can be seen the ribbed stone domes from tombs of several Mamluk amirs and princesses from the fourteenth and fifteenth centuries. However, most of the tombs here are more recent.

The Citadel walls seen from the north-west. The towers at the far left are from the twelfth century, the exquisite Mosque of Suleiman Pasha with its Turkish-style multiple domes is from the sixteenth. The walls in the foreground enclose a palace built by Muhammad Ali, founder of the dynasty that ruled Egypt from 1806 to 1952. The palace once housed the Pasha's harem; it now contains a military museum. The poor quarters that can be seen pressing up to the fortress walls may have a reputation for lawlessness, but they enjoy a terrific view over the city.

Densely packed tombs in the Southern Cemetery, with fourteenth- and fifteenth-century domes and minarets. The classic Cairo minaret has three stages: square, octagonal and round. Pencil-shaped Turkish minarets became fashionable after the Ottoman Turks conquered Egypt in 1517, but modern mosques have reverted to the native style. The square apartment blocks in the background are low-income public housing built in the 1960s.

On Fridays it is customary for Egyptian women to visit the graves of their relatives. For this reason, many tombs have courtyards and rocfed rooms to accommodate visitors. Here we see a poorer cemetery, with many of the graves planted in the open.

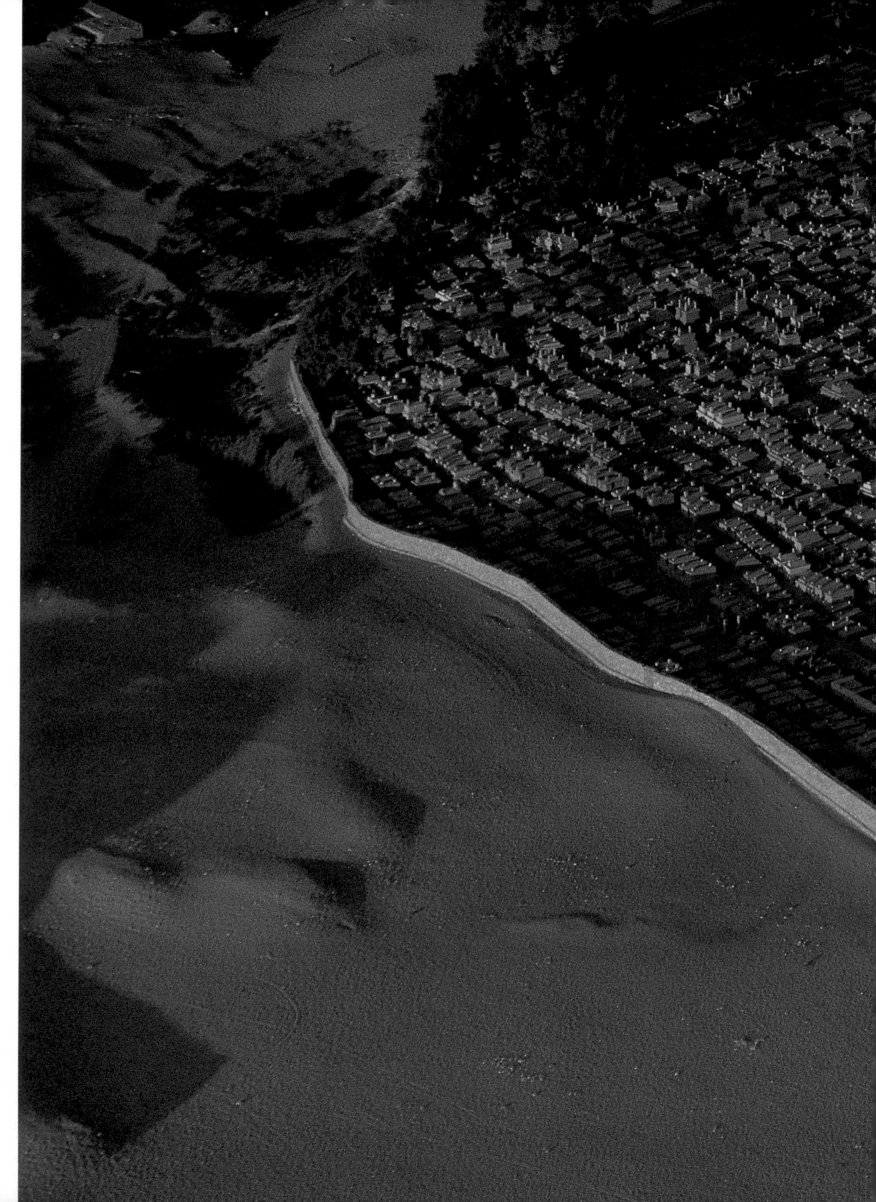

Right next to the Pyramids, on the edge of the desert, sprawls a cemetery that exhibits much more modest, modern funeral architecture.

The twin minarets of the fifteenth-century Mosque of Muayyad stand atop the eleventh-century gate known as Bab Zuwayla in the heart of Cairo's medieval quarter. The gate originally fortified the walled imperial court of the Fatimid caliphs, but over the centuries Cairo spread both inside and outside the walls, making the gate obsolete. The gardens of the Mosque of Muayyad provide a welcome patch of green amid the crowded bazaars of the district.

Another of Cairo's eleventh-century gates. Bab al Nasr, has two square towers. The roof in the left foreground covers the eleventh-century Mosque of Al Hakim. The adjacent building, whose roof is sadly in need of repair, is a fifteenth-century caravanserai. For the convenience of traveling merchants it was built just inside the city walls.

The Mosque of Ahmed Ibn Tulun is the largest of all the open-courtyard mosques in Cairo. It is the only structure that survives from the new city built by Ibn Tulun in the ninth century, a city that was razed to the ground when the Abbasids of Baghdad reconquered Egypt. The perfect order of the mosque's interior contrasts with the bustle of the street outside, suggesting the spiritual peace of Islam. The unusual spiral minaret reflects the Mesopotamian fashion of the time. Scholars speculate that the unusually high crenellations atop the wall were meant to look like ranks of soldiers in silhouette. In the foreground are the domes and courtyard of the fourteenth-century Mosque of Sarghatmish, its smaller scale reflecting the increased density of the city at that time.

The Mosque of Amr Ibn al Asi is named for the Muslim general whose army brought Islam to Egypt in A.D. 641. It is the oldest mosque in Africa. Repeated renovations have obscured the original construction, but the building's simple decoration still reflects the asceticism of early Islam. Once in the center of the city, the mosque now stands among tombs.

Saladdin Square below the Citadel is lined with grand monuments. The square was formerly a polo ground and hippodrome for Mamluk horsemen. The arches of the ruined fifteenth-century Maristan or Hospital al Muayyad are visible in the far right background. On the far left can be seen the unusual spiral ribbed dome of the fourteenth-century Mosque of Ilgay al Yusufi.

The madrasa of Sultan Hassan (1356) was meant to have four minarets the same height as the one in the foreground – which is the highest in Cairo. But plans had to be scaled back due to the high cost of the building's interior decor. Part of the expense was said to have been met with the estates of plague victims who had left no heirs. After nearly bankrupting the state to build his monument, Sultan Hassan was murdered before it could be completed.

These two mosques are painted in the traditional ablaq or candy-stripes, a fashion imported from Andalusia in the fourteenth century. The Mahmoudiya Mosque in the foreground dates from just after the Ottoman conquest and combines a Turkish-style minaret with typically Cairene features. The mosque in the background, built in 1503 by the commander of Sultan al Ghuri's cavalry, is a masterpiece of Mamluk architecture. It is set ingeniously on three levels, but the lines of the façade carefully conceal the sloping site. The carved-stone dome is one of the finest in Cairo.

The Mosque of
Muhammad Ali
dominates Cairo from
its perch in the Citadel.
Although its nineteenth-
century builder
challenged Turkish rule
over Egypt, and indeed
would have defeated
the Ottomans had
Europe not intervened,
he chose to build his
great mosque in the
style of Istanbul.
The lower façade is
paneled with alabaster.
The dome is over fifty
meters high.

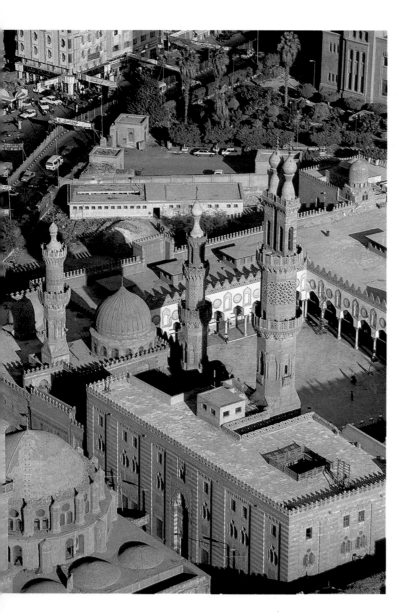

The courtyard seen here is the heart of Al Azhar University, said to be the oldest in the world. The arcades date from its founding in 970 as an institute for Islamic theology. Successive rulers wishing to show off their piety have built additions such as these three minarets. Since the 1952 revolution Al Azhar has been expanded into a full-blown university, but it still retains its status as the foremost center for orthodox Sunni scholarship in the Islamic world. The area (right) between the Mosque of Al Azhar in the foreground and the Mosque of Hussein in the background is one of the busiest in Cairo. The largest of Cairo's popular saints' days revolves around the Mosque of Hussein, where the head of the prophet's martyred grandson is said to be buried. The low roofs to the left of the mosque cover the tiny alleyways of the Khan al Khalili, Cairo's great bazaar for jewelry, knick-knacks and antiques.

The Mosque of Al Hakim was recently renovated by the Bohhra, a Shiite Indian sect that traces its ancestry back to the eleventh-century Fatimid Caliph Al Hakim. This Egyptian ruler had a reputation for whimsy and madness, on one occasion banning the sale of women's shoes. Believers in Al Hakim's divinity founded the Druze sect in Lebanon. Note the two unusual minarets. The far wall of the mosque forms part of the defensive walls of Cairo, another of the gates of which — Bab al Futuh — can be seen on the left.

The Islamic Museum, founded in the late nineteenth century, houses a rare collection of Islamic art from as far afield as India and Andalusia. Particularly impressive are the Cairene glass and metalwork of the fourteenth and fifteenth centuries. Port Said Street, with the tram passing along it, was formerly a canal that ran through the center of the medieval city.

Highrise apartments in the district of Doqqi on the west bank of the Nile give Cairo a strikingly modern look. Skyrocketing land prices and an ever-growing population have pushed the height of buildings dizzyingly upwards since the 1960s. The Cairo Tower, seen in the background, has a revolving restaurant with a superb view. On either side of the tower, across the river, stand the TV Building and the new Foreign Ministry complex.

The so-called Golden Mile, where luxury hotels and apartments line Cairo's Nile-side Corniche. At sunset the river takes on an unnaturally healthy-looking blue tint. Beyond the façade of buildings hums the bustle of central Cairo. Seekers of peace gravitate to the sailboats and cafes of the riverbank.

THE NILE

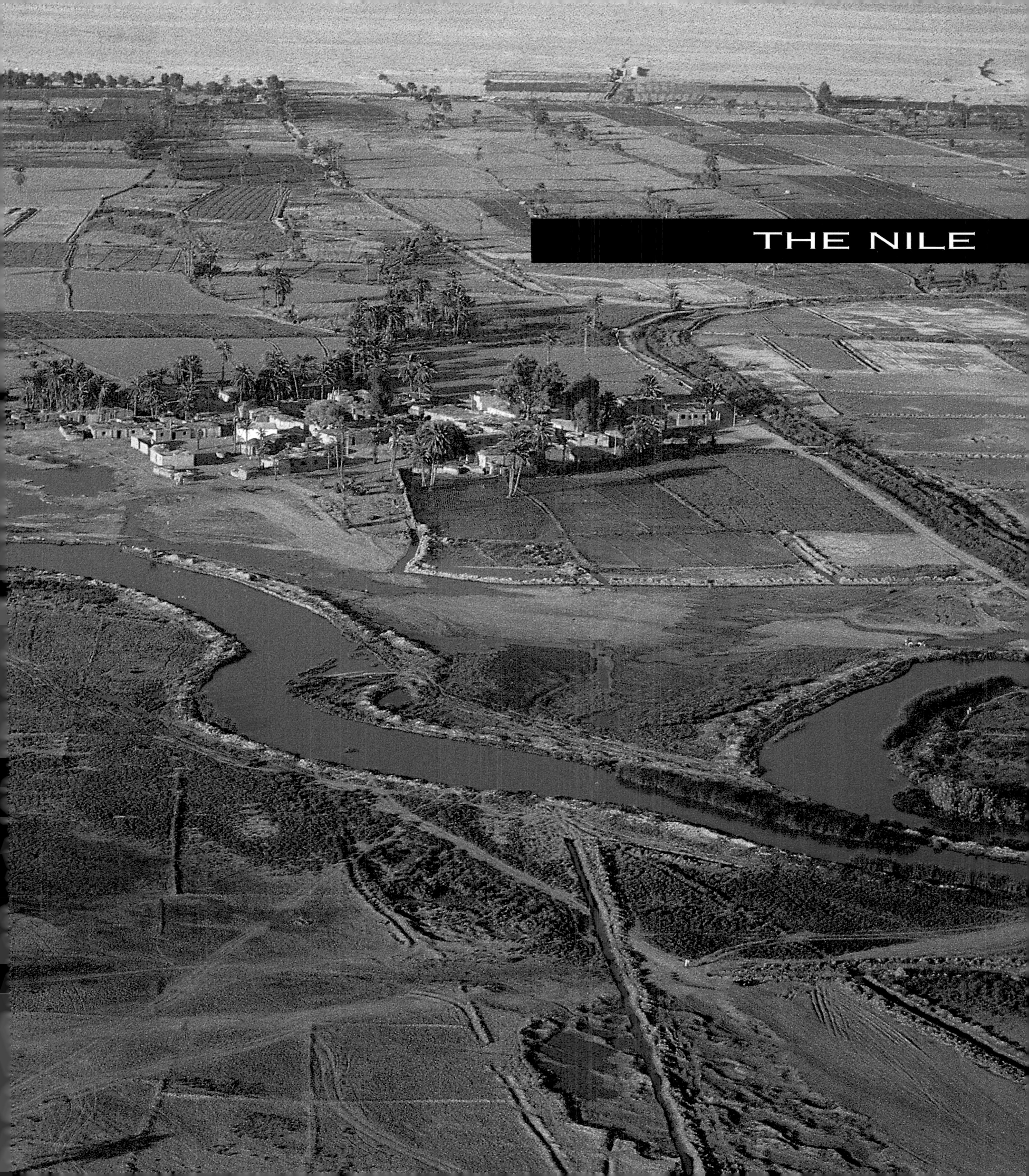

As one looks down from a traffic-rattled Cairo bridge, it is hard to recall that the placid stream below, so tame and even tired-looking, is none other than the fabled Nile, that longest and most ancient of known rivers, whose source remained a mystery a mere century-and-a-half ago. It is hard to imagine that every murky drop has seen the still-wild depths of Africa, has lingered in mountain lakes and crashed over jungle waterfalls, has slinked through civil wars and percolated in swamps and deserts. Or that somewhere along the way every cupful has been touched by man, has watered his fields and driven his turbines.

It is not enough to echo the Greek traveler Herodotus, who called Egypt "the gift of the Nile." True, without its umbilical link to the green African highlands Egypt would be as dull a patch of desert as neighboring Arabia. Migrating birds would lose their way without the Nile's guiding shimmer. People would choose another corner of the Mediterranean in which to build their civilizations. But the Nile has meant much more than this. Its moods and its constants underly the very essence of what is Egyptian. The Nile's story is Egypt's story.

In the eternity before the completion of the High Dam at Aswan in 1970, the annual rhythm of flood and recess stamped every aspect of Egyptian life. Beginning in midsummer, rain in the Ethiopian highlands swelled the river. By September the water stretched from desert to desert across the valley. The Delta became a lake, as the Greek geographer Strabo described it in the first century: "But at the time of the rising of the Nile, the whole country is covered, and resembles a sea, except the inhabited spots, which are situated upon natural hills or mounds; and considerable cities and villages appear like islands in the distant prospect. The water, after having continued on the ground more than forty days in summer, then subsides by degrees, in the same manner as it rose. In sixty days the plain is entirely exposed to view, and dries up."

As it receded the river left a thick residue from the silt eroded off mountainsides half a continent away. This enriching alluvium gave Egypt its ancient name, Kemet, meaning the Black Land, so distinguishable from the surrounding yellowed wastes. The Nile silt also gave Egypt its wealth. It is hardly surprising that agriculture should have flourished early here, where a farmer could plant by merely scattering seeds as the flood receded. As Herodotus wrote in the fifth century B.C.: "These people get their harvests with less labor than anyone else in the world....They merely wait for the river of its own accord to flood their fields; then, when the water has receded, each farmer sows his plot, turns the pigs into it to tread in the seed, and then waits for the harvest."

Dependable inundations enabled the Ancient Egyptians to undertake some of their most ambitious projects. At Aswan stone-cutters wedged plugs of dry wood into the riverside granite. When the flood covered the

An Egyptian village, with its mudbrick houses strung along a palm-studded canal bank, the domed tomb of a local holy man in the center, fields stretching away on either side. Note the rich blackness of the soil. PRECEDING PAGES: An Egyptian scene that has remained unchanged for thousands of years: flat, irrigated farmland with the desert beyond. This is the man-made oasis of Al Fayum, where channels from the Nile meander down to Lake Qarun, which lies below sea-level. Even in a thirsty land like Egypt too much water can be a problem. Poor drainage results in water-logging and patches of salinity.

More and more, Egypt is coming to look like the top of this photograph rather than the bottom. Lush fields stop abruptly at the edge of Al Fayum City, a swelling provincial capital with all the urban troubles of Cairo, though on a smaller scale. Even from the air Egyptian cabbages, at the lower right, appear gigantic!

boulders the wood expanded and cracked the hard stone, making it easy to haul away for fashioning into obelisks and the like. Engineers of the Twelfth Dynasty created the rich artificial oasis of Al Fayum by channeling floodwaters into a desert depression to form the lake now known as Qarun.

The Pharaohs of the Old Kingdom, powerful as they may have been, never could have gathered the manpower to stack millions of blocks of stone on a desert ridge if it weren't for the fact that when the whole valley disappeared under the rising river, no farm work was possible. Nor could they have moved pyramid-weights of stone unless the high Nile reached as far as the quarries at the desert's edge.

The flood had other effects, too, as Strabo points out: "An exact and minute division of the country was required by the frequent confusion of boundaries occasioned at the time of the rise of the Nile…which…obliterates marks by which the property of one person is distinguished from that of another. It was consequently necessary to measure the land repeatedly. Hence it is said geometry originated here." By the same token, the Greek might have noted that land disputes increased the need for a central government, which may explain why Egypt developed a strong state, with kings and the inevitable bureaucrats, so early on. Also, since everyone lived on the river's banks, the country was easy to control. It is no coincidence that Egypt's southern border has traditionally been at Aswan, above which a number of waterfalls or cataracts render boat passage difficult.

The Nile's influences have been subtler, too. The Ancient Egyptian's vision of the cosmos, which included the sun traveling in a boat across the horizon, was drawn from the country's landscape. Egyptian attitudes to the world, even today, are shaped by the insularity and crowding of valley life. The outside world is a source of amusement, wonder and sometimes fear. Tellingly, Egyptians call the low desert hills that hem the valley so closely on either side Al Gabal – the Mountains – as if they were some fearsome and insurmountable obstacle.

After millennia in the arduous service of mankind, it is perhaps not surprising that the river, now dammed and pumped and siphoned for irrigation and superseded by bridges and roads for transport, should be taken for granted. The modern Egyptians hold

A small herd of camels awaits its fate. Camels are still used for labor, but more often are raised for meat and hides.

no celebrations in its honor. Their only praise comes in the dry form of the water-level statistics announced yearly by the Minister of Irrigation.

Three thousand years ago priests appeased the river with prayers like this one, probably composed for an inundation festival: "Praise to thee O Nile, that issueth from the earth and cometh to nourish Egypt. Of hidden nature, a darkness in the daytime….That watereth the meadows, he that Re hath created to nourish all cattle. That giveth drink to the desert places, which are far from water; it is his dew that falleth from heaven….

Venerable riverboats
bring to mind the
charm of Nile cruises
as they used to be.
In the old days visitors
spent several weeks on
the Nile. Now cabin
cruisers made of
aluminum and glass
churn from Aswan to
Luxor in three days.
The boat at top was not
a tour vessel; it was a
private house-boat
complete with a
glassed-in observation
deck and several
staterooms.

A felucca pick-up carries a donkey and a heavy load of bricks as well as passengers. The lateen rig, broad beam, low draught and heavy rudder are all typical of Nile craft. The river was made for sailing: The current flows to the north and the wind almost always blows to the south. These days, however, most feluccas are in the tourist trade.

If he be (low) the whole land is in terror and great and small lament ....When he riseth, the land is in exultation and everybody is in joy. All jaws begin to laugh and every tooth is revealed....When the Nile floodeth, offering is made to thee, cattle are slaughtered for thee, a great oblation is made for thee. Fowl are fattened for thee, antelopes are hunted for thee in the desert. Good is recompensed unto thee.... Thou art verdant, O Nile, thou art verdant."

The dunes at Aswan drop right down into the river. This villa belongs to the widow of one of the Aga Khans. Sailboats carry visitors to his impressive tomb, which stands atop the hill behind the house. Every day a fresh red rose is placed on the white marble cenotaph.

It is thought that on occasion the ancients turned to much more dramatic means than prayer. Virgins may once have been hurled off the cliffs near Aswan to propitiate the river. Until the nineteenth century A.D. the biggest festival in Cairo marked the cutting of a dam built annually to hold back floodwaters from the canal that ran through the city. Perhaps in emulation of the human sacrifice, an effigy known as the "bride of the Nile" was placed before the dam to be washed away by the current.

The Ancient Egyptians had good reason to pay the gods their due. The Bible's Seven Years of Famine recurred often. A pharaonic inscription at Edfu in Upper Egypt records one occasion: "By very great misfortune the Nile has not come forth for a period of seven years. Grain has been scarce and there have been no vegetables or anything else for the people to eat." The inscription goes on to say that the king ordered the offering of rich sacrifices. Even in recent years the river has fallen dangerously low. To escape the effects of the Ethiopian drought of the early 1980s, Egypt nearly exhausted the Aswan Reservoir, without which Egyptians too may have starved.

Nor was drought the only danger. Sir William Willcocks, a British hydrologist, gave this graphic description of a raging flood: "The terror reigning over the whole country during a very high flood is very striking....In a settlement north of Mansoura in 1887 I witnessed a scene which must have once been more common than it is today. The news that the riverbank had been breached spread fast through the village. The villagers rushed out onto the banks with their children, their cattle, and everything they possessed. The confusion was indescribable. A narrow bank crowded with buffaloes, children, poultry and household furniture. The women assembled around the local saint's tomb, beating their breasts, kissing the tomb and uttering loud cries, and every five minutes a gang of men running into the crowd and carrying off the first thing they could lay hands on wherewith to close the breach. The fellaheen, meanwhile...stood shoulder to shoulder across the escaping water, and with the aid of torn-off doors and windows and Indian cornstalks, closed the breach. They were only just in time."

The twin dangers of flood and famine, in addition to the potential rewards of water management in providing for year-round irrigation, led the rulers of Egypt to seek control over the Nile. With the introduction of cotton in the 1800s, it was realized that investment in irrigation could bring material rewards. From that time onward, new canals, barrages and reservoirs were built. Cultivation intensified and increasing amounts of land came into use. But in spite of the Delta Barrage north of Cairo, the Low Dam at Aswan and other engineering works, the river remained capricious.

Looking for an issue that would symbolize a resurgent Egypt, the leaders of the 1952 revolution proclaimed that a dam would be built – a dam that would once and for all free the country from nature's whimsy. As one Western scholar phrased it, "Egypt's erstwhile divine gift was to be appropriated by central state authority." A postcard that was printed at the time of the announcement captured its significance to Egyptians: It showed a sword-wielding President Nasser slashing at a dragon-headed flood poised to ravish a prostrate, buxom Egypt.

The High Dam at Aswan has wreaked a greater transformation in Egyptian life than perhaps any single construction has brought to any other country. But the dam has brought curses as well as blessings. Farmers now rely on man-made fertilizers rather than natural silt, and the chemicals poison fish and birds. Irrigation is now year-round rather than seasonal. This development brings higher yields, but it also requires more work and causes water-logging of the soil. Partly because of the dam, bilharzia, a debilitating water-born disease, has spread. Weeds that the flood would have washed away now clog canals. Where the Nile reaches the Mediterranean, colossal dikes scar the coastline; the Delta, once buttressed by a yearly deposit of fresh silt, is now being eaten away by the sea.

Ancient monuments also have suffered from the dam. The pressure of the Aswan Reservoir and the extension of irrigation have raised the water table, which has pushed corrosive salts to the surface. These feast on the limestone blocks from which Egypt's greatest monuments are built. The marble inlay in Cairo mosques puckers and crumbles from the walls. Columns in the Luxor Temple have begun to lean precariously. Even the Sphinx is sponging up the deadly liquid.

Of ancient Nubia – the land between Aswan and the Sudanese border – all that survives are the great temples of Philae, Kalabsha and Abu Simbel. At enormous cost they were dismantled and hoisted to dry land. The rest of the country, along with its heritage, lies under the waters of the High Dam Lake. The dark-skinned Nubians, with their own distinct languages, architecture and culture, have been subsumed into urban Egypt.

In its last and perhaps final chapter, the story of the Nile has turned as predictable as the flow of water from a kitchen tap. And so the Egyptians have turned their interest elsewhere. After millennia of confinement in the valley, they have begun to push outward into the desert, reclaiming land and building roads and cities where they had never ventured before.

While washing pots and pans in the river this girl stopped to watch a passing helicopter. Many villages lack running water, and the river carries bilharzia as well as industrial pollution. Brightly colored dresses like the one seen here cre the fashion in villages.

Lake Nasser, formed when the High Dam was completed in 1970, has swamped the desert over thousands of square kilometers. The lake acts as a huge evaporation pan. Under its waters lie the lost monuments and villages of Nubia. Efforts to utilize the lake for fishing, and to make use of the rich silt building up on its bottom, have as yet borne little fruit.

A fast current, granite boulders and numerous islands make the Nile at Aswan picturesque, but also a waterway requiring considerable skill to navigate. Aswan is the traditional southernmost point in Egypt. Upriver from here a number of cataracts or rapids made the Nile impassable; now the two great dams on the river block the way. At left is a luxury hotel on one of the islands.

The houses in this Upper Egyptian village have upturned corners in the style of nearby ancient temples. Under the high-tension wires in the background – which probably carry power from the High Dam – stretches a field of sugar-cane. The tall, dense crop makes an ideal hideout for outlaws. Opium and marijuana are often grown secretly in patches amid the cane.

The aerial view gives rural Egypt an orderliness that is less apparent from the ground. Here we see how tightly packed the village houses are, how minutely divided the fields. The yellow areas are newly harvested cane fields; some patches have already been burned to prepare the soil for replanting. The dark green crops are clover for the animals and vegetables for human consumption.

A riverside village in Upper Egypt. The dun-colored brick creates an earthy glow at sunset. The proliferation of palms suggests that these houses have recently supplanted fields. Note the reinforced pillars protruding from some roofs. The population explosion is so intense that home-owners plan ahead – they build supports for additional floors.

This little boat-yard in Esna still builds traditional wooden feluccas, but many are fitted now with outboard motors. In the jumble of buildings behind, the mosque stands out as a single point of splendor. Village habits persist in the poverty of Egypt's provincial cities.

This village perched on the edge of the desert near Aswan is distinctively Nubian, and it is one of the few villages of this African people not flooded by the High Dam. Nubian houses are spaced far apart, with large, uncluttered open courtyards. Mudbrick domes and vaults help keep the interiors of the dwellings cool. In contrast to Egyptian fellaheen, the Nubians pay careful attention to decor. As we see here, most of the houses are painted a stark, clean white.

Village houses near Luxor give an idea of the Egyptian farmer's closeness to Mother Earth. Even in villages, houses must be packed close together to conserve productive farmland.

Tourism makes its presence felt in the villages near Luxor. Here a local artist shows off his talent in a variety of styles. He has created obelisks and a pharaonic doorway; classic folk images like the lion, the swan and the water-bearing girl; traditional paintings celebrating a relative's pilgrimage to Mecca, and finally some modern patriotic icons like the Egyptian flag. The Arabic calligraphy bears religious sayings.

This village lies at the foot of the desert cliffs west of Luxor, which conceal thousands of ancient tombs, including the Valley of the Kings. Known as Gurna, it has been infamous for centuries as a haven for tomb-robbers. Some families' houses have been found to sit atop extensive tunnels used to pillage their long-dead ancestors' graves. Government efforts to resettle the villagers have failed.

The province of Qena north of Luxor is a center for traditional pottery. Here banks of new water-jars dry in the sun. In the background is an open-pit kiln. So abundant is pottery in Qena that it is even used for building. Here quarters for farm animals are made of clay jars mortared with mud. These neat brick row-houses strangely evoke working-class suburbs in London or some other Western city. The simple decoration, however, suggests ancient Rome.

Village children – the girls in bright dresses, the boys in long galabeyas – do much of the farmwork at harvest time. Increasingly, modern machinery takes more of the load. But note the numbers of goats, sheep and donkeys here. A third of Egypt's precious land is used to keep them fed.

If it weren't for the faint outline of a television aerial there would be nothing to place this scene in the twentieth century. This impoverished Egyptian homestead could be anywhere else in Africa or straight out of the pharaonic past. A round earthen stove is used for making bread. On the mudbrick cottage's roof, red peppers dry in the sun.

Egypt has pinned its hopes for future food self-sufficiency on huge desert land-reclamation programs. This project north-east of Cairo uses a pivoting irrigation boom to spray crops. Drip irrigation, which is now gaining popularity, has proved to consume much less of the Nile's precious water.

A vision of Egypt's future north of Cairo. The desert is being pushed back. Bulldozers level sand dunes. Plastic sheeting covers high-value crops fed by drip irrigation and destined for export. But despite the effort expended in reclamation, nearly as much fertile land is lost every year to expanding cities.

Straw and fodder are stored on village roofs, as in this typical canal-side hamlet. Fields are often divided into long thin strips, partly because under Islamic law inherited property must be carefully partitioned among relatives. Often a settlement like this one will belong to a single extended family.

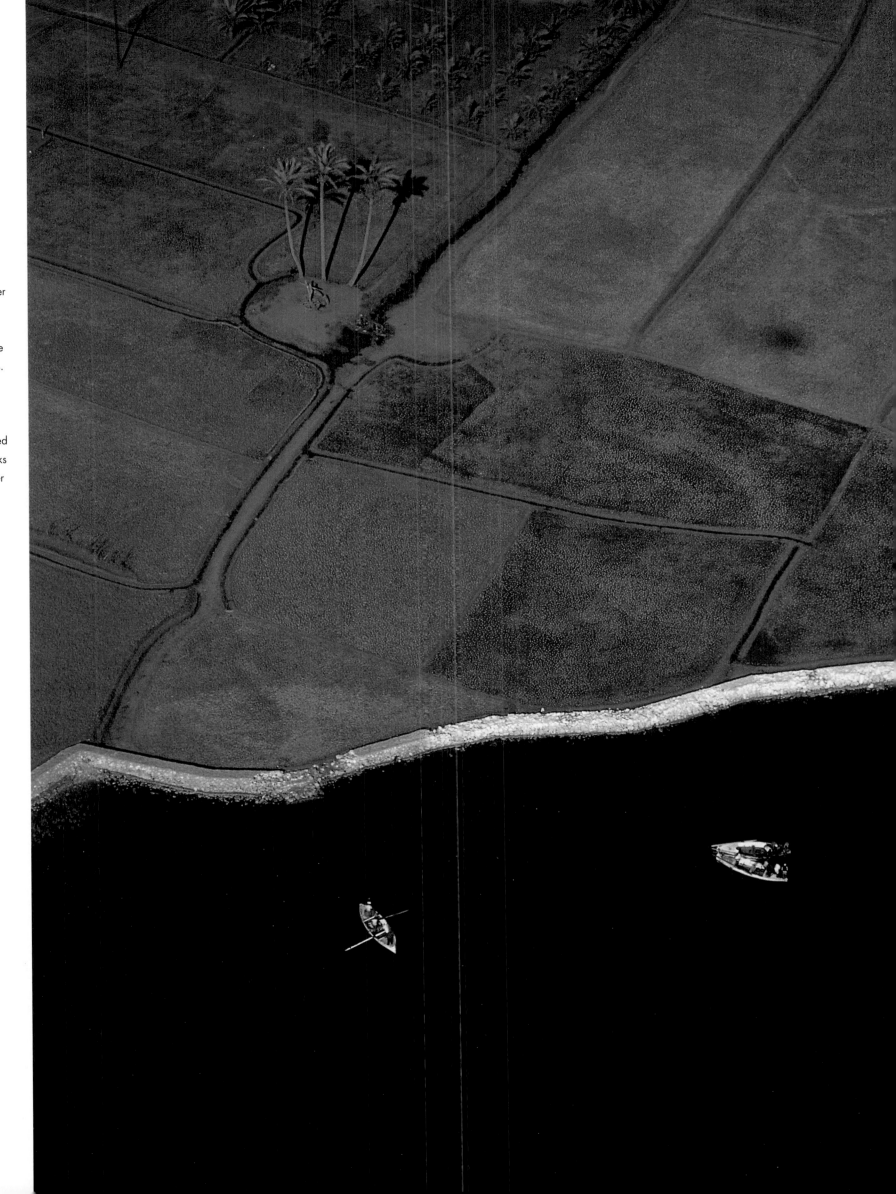

The river-bank in the Delta, where the currents are gentler, is more stable than further south. Here we see fishing boats and, above, an idyllic grove of feathery date palms. A saqiya or water-wheel rests next to them. A blindfolded water-buffalo is tethered to the wheel, and walks in circles to raise water to the level of the smaller channels that feed the fields.

Farmland like this, said to be the most fertile in the world, stretches to the horizon in the Delta. Egypt's average farm measures less than one-and-a-quarter acres. To make up for the small size of their plots, farmers grow three crops a year. Irrigation water is rationed according to strict, age-old regimes that give each farmer just as much as he needs. FOLLOWING PAGES: A dawn mist in the Nile Valley heightens the drama of the desert escarpment. Although the cliffs are mere hills, Egyptians refer to them as Al Gabal – the Mountains.

Vacationers at the
small inland sea of
Lake Qarun in Al
Fayum. Created by
runoff water from the
Nile, the lake has
turned salty over its
4,000-year lifespan.
The Ancient Egyptians
for a time preserved a
sanctuary for crocodiles
here. Special priests
are said to have hand-
fed them milk and
honey. The reptiles
have now retreated
outside Egypt's borders.

A lake-shore village. Salinification and pollution from agricultural chemicals have greatly affected Qarun's fish catch. Traditional rowing boats with flat-bladed oars lie idle. The crescent-shaped lake has an unusual feature: One shore is green, the other desert.

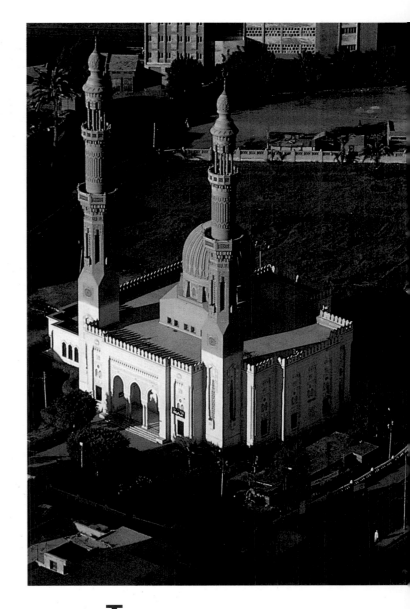

The Bahr Yusuf, a channel branching from the Nile, winds through the middle of Al Fayum City. The man-made river then divides into a half-dozen fingers that spread through the surrounding oasis of two million inhabitants. The scheme to utilize the depression now filled by Lake Qarun for draining excess Nile water is thought to have been executed under the Twelfth-Dynasty Pharaoh Amenemhet I. Like most modern Egyptian mosques, this one in Al Fayum City emulctes the Mamluk style of medieval Cairo. The minarets are in three stages, capped by a columned pavilion But whereas in older mosques domes always cover a tomb, here the dome roofs the main prayer hall.

The need for fresh land has pushed Egyptian farmers to their country's seacoasts as well as its deserts. Here patches of cultivation are being reclaimed from a salt lake on the Mediterrahean coast. Fertile Nile silt is trucked in to improve the soil. This land will someday be as green as the neighboring Delta.

Much of the flat northern Delta lies only centimeters above sea-level. Tracts of salt-marsh are walled with earth and allowed to evaporate. The salt leaves a white residue, but over time can be leached out of the soil. Places such as this were uninhabitable until the flow of the Nile was fully controlled.

Salt pans, like giant inkwells, form a palette of colors. Here we see ochres and oranges; there are also pinks, purples and greens in these extensive works near Port Said.

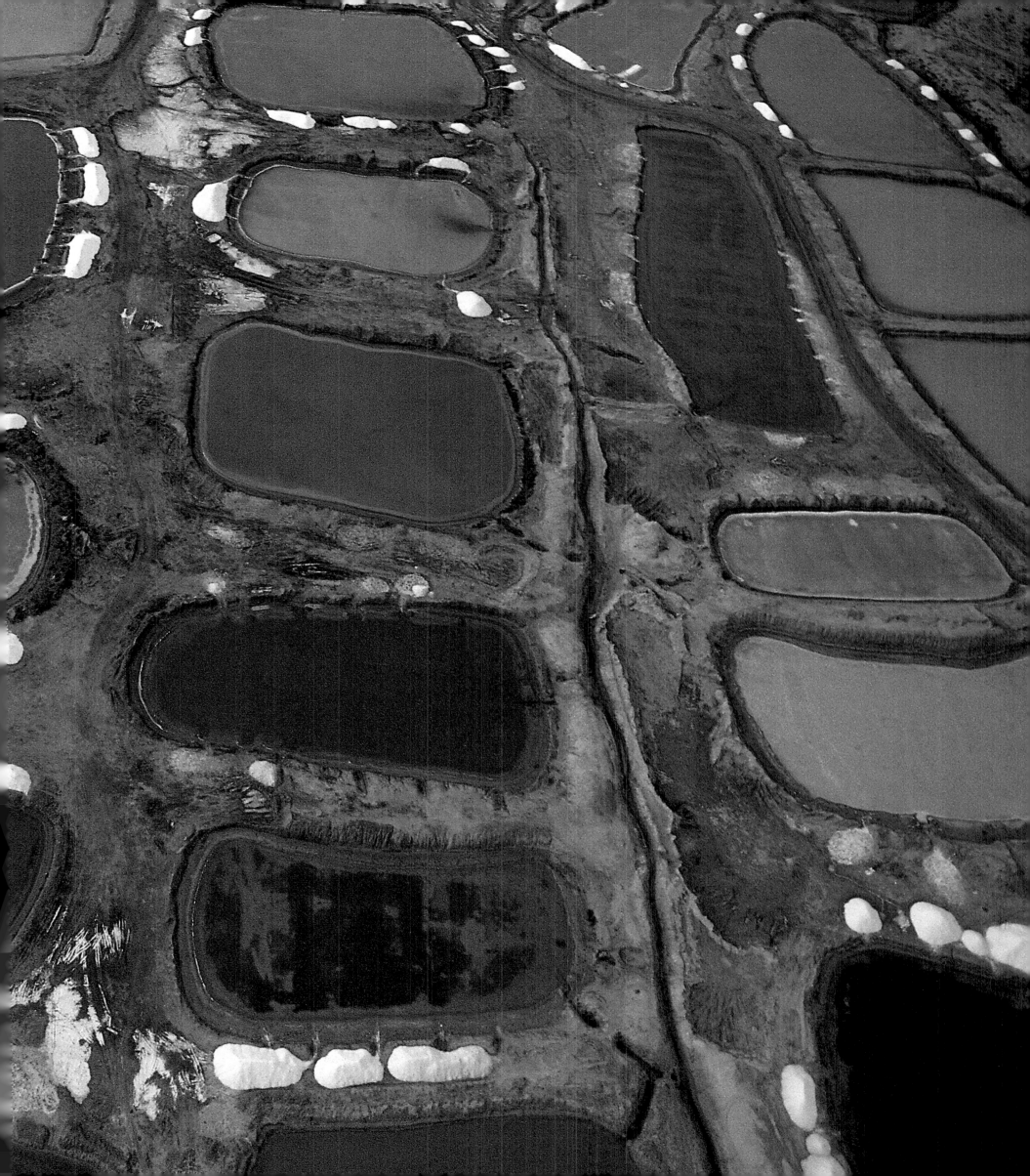

THE DESERT

Deserts are barren, forbidding. There is no water, of course, and the scathing light whites out color and contour. In the long summer there is no shade or other shelter from the skull-swelling heat, and when a cooling wind does blow, it pitches up bales of dust and grit. The winter cold is sudden, dry and piercing. Scorpions squat under every rock. Snakes slither in the endless sand. Small wonder then that only one in twenty-five Egyptians ventures to live in the waterless waste that fills all but a fraction of the country's surface. The Nile Valley is the most crowded patch of real estate on earth. The surrounding desert is one of the emptiest. It is as if all the French occupied only the immediate banks of the Loire, or all the Russians clung solely to the Volga.

To the ancients the desert was alien, the Red Land as opposed to their own Black Land by the river banks. It was the abode of the wicked God Seth who murdered his brother Osiris. And so the Egyptians populated it with tombs: the pyramids at Giza, Saqqara and elsewhere; the valleys of the Kings and Queens and Nobles at Thebes; the necropolises for mummified crocodiles, birds, cats and baboons.

But if it was a place of death for Egyptians, the desert also was a place of doom for invaders. Insulating Egypt from the surrounding lands, it was the country's natural defense. Compared to its rival Mesopotamia, where a bewildering array of civilizations overlapped and clashed, Ancient Egypt was rarely subjected to conquest.

Even after the introduction of the hardy camel sometime in the first millennium B.C., invaders seldom penetrated the desert barrier, which in times of good government was reinforced by a string of fortifications. During Saladdin's time, captive Crusaders were put to work building the forts of Qalaat al Gundi in the middle of the Sinai Peninsula and Gezirat Faraon on the Gulf of Aqaba. Right down to modern times the deserts of Sinai and Libya have witnessed battles. East of the Suez Canal wrecked Israeli tanks rust in the open sand, victims of the wars of 1956, 1967 and 1973. West of Alexandria straying goats still set off the occasional land mine left from the Axis advance to Al Alamein in the Second World War, when Rommel the Desert Fox nearly succeeded in capturing the Suez Canal and cutting off Allied oil supplies.

Uninviting though the desert may be it has, like that other fear-some barrier the sea, tempted the adventurous among the living, and from the earliest times. Prehistoric rock drawings far from the fertile valley depict hunting grounds for elephants, ostrich, lions and other African game that flourished in the desert in cooler ages. By the Third Dynasty, around 2600 B.C., Egyptians were mining turquoise and copper deep in the Sinai Peninsula. Between the Nile and the Red Sea they found gold in such abundance that a foreign king wrote the Eighteenth-Dynasty Pharaoh

Having no cover of vegetation, desert landscapes are miniature geography lessons. This large wadi in the Eastern Desert is joined by dozens of tributaries, each of which has cut its own valley out of the barren earth. PRECEDING PAGES: Time and water have eroded these snaking wadis – seasonal water channels – out of a flat gravel plateau east of the Nile.

A baked stretch of land in the Eastern Desert. Distance is hard to judge in the desert: There is nothing to measure it against. From the top to the bottom of this photograph could be one kilometer or ten. After a winter rain, wadis like this one come to life as dangerous torrents. Flash floods wash away desert roads. Even in the desert, the unwary have been known to drown.

Loose sand retains a print of water flow from one rare rainfall until the next. The geology of the Sinai Peninsula is very varied. Rock erodes at different rates, depending on its hardness, exposing streaks and blotches of color. The desolate aspect of the Sinai belies the fact that it is one of Egypt's more habitable deserts. Local bedouin still scratch out a living in the Sinai, herding goats and camels.

Amenhotep III, "Let my brother send gold in great quantity, for in my brother's land gold is plentiful as dust." From the hills of Nubia came amethyst and cornelian. From the Wadi el Natrun west of the Delta came natron, an important tool of the mummification trade. The deserts also concealed beryl, emeralds, garnet, onyx and agate.

For the discerning Romans Egypt was the sole source of highly prized imperial porphyry. The dense roseate stone was hauled from a barren mountaintop near the Red Sea. Then it was dragged a hundred kilometers overland and shipped downriver all the way to Rome. Fueling the fashion for portraiture, it was the favored stone for busts of emperors and nobles.

Since Paleolithic times men have occupied what Strabo described as "certain inhabited tracts, which are surrounded by extensive deserts, and appear like islands in the sea." The five greater oases of the Egyptian Sahara, wind-sculpted depressions where underwater aquifers come to the surface, have seen their fortunes oscillate. In dynastic times the oasis of Kharga nearest the Nile was a place of exile, a sort of Egyptian gulag. But despite their isolation, Kharga and the other oases boasted temples and sumptuous villas that would have graced any pharaonic town. Their wines and dates were prized. In the Roman era the oasis of Dakhla was quite cosmopolitan, as shown by recently excavated philosophic and religious manuscripts in Greek, Syriac and Aramaic.

In the Middle Ages desert raiders from Libya and Sudan challenged central government control of the oases. Like the islanders of the Mediterranean, oasis folk built dense walled towns for self-defense. Some of these mudbrick hives, such as the old city of Siwa, have crumbled. But others have survived. At Dakhla the villages of Al Qasr and Balat preserve their warrens of whitewashed, hand-molded streets.

The oases had some famous visitors. Cambyses, the cruel Persian king who conquered Egypt in the sixth century B.C., set his heart on capturing Siwa, the distant oasis of Ammon. More than a century later Herodotus described what happened: "The force which was sent against the Ammonians started from Thebes with guides, and can be traced as far as the town of Oasis [Kharga] which…is seven days' journey across the sand from Thebes. The place is known in Greek as the Island of the Blessed. General report has it that the army got as far as this, but of its subsequent fate there is no news whatever. It never reached the Ammonians and it never returned to Egypt. There is, however, a story told by the Ammonians themselves and by others who heard it from them, that when the men had left Oasis, and in their march across the desert had reached a point about midway between the town and the Ammonian border, a southerly wind of extreme violence drove the sand over them in heaps as they were taking their midday meal, so that they disappeared forever."

A small chapel at the summit of Mount Sinai marks the spot where Moses is believed to have met his maker. The site, just above the Monastery of Saint Catherine, draws thousands of visitors. Many scramble up the steep path in the early morning to catch the spectacular wrap-around view of rose-colored peaks at dawn.

Desert highways link Cairo to Egypt's oases and coasts. This half-built one goes to Al Fayum and replaces an older road, part of which can be seen at the top of the photograph. The bulldozer's scratches look tiny in the immensity of the wasteland. This part of the Western Desert is flat, featureless and uninhabited – except by passing cars.

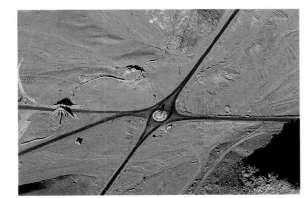

This desert crossroads, empty of vehicles, is at the village of Saint Catherine in the Sinai. The spider-like structure is the grandiose gateway to a hotel.

A later conqueror also yearned to reach Siwa, but for more pacific reasons. Having subdued much of the known world, Alexander the Great made the desert trek to the oasis to visit its famous oracle, which obligingly informed him that he was the son of God. Legend has it that though his train lost its way, a flight of heaven-sent swallows guided it to safety.

Bandits and outlaws traditionally sought refuge in Egypt's deserts. The most famous was Moses, who is said to have held out in Sinai for forty years. In later times Christians fleeing Roman persecution and heretics banished by the orthodox church fled to remote caves and built fortified monasteries. Among them were sects of Gnostics whose radical theologies, ridiculed and suppressed by the later church, only recently came to light with the discovery of the Nag Hammadi scrolls. In their desert isolation the early anchorites regimented their lives around prayer and debate. Strangers coming to their walled fortresses could enter only by being winched up in baskets.

To this day smugglers of antiquities, narcotics and arms hole up in desert wadis and mountains. But for at least the past millennium the true sons of the desert have been the Arab bedouin. Freewheeling and warlike, their character contrasts with the stolid and fearful nature of the fellaheen just as the open desert contrasts with the crowded valley. Although the urban lifestyle has pushed far into their territory, the Egyptian bedouin still carry a reputation best described in a century-old classic, Charles Doughty's *Travels in Arabia Deserta*: "The Bedu toil not (say they), that is not bodily; but their spirits are made weary with incessant apprehension of their enemies, and their flesh with continual thirst and hunger. The necessitous lives of the Aarab may hardly reach to a virtuous mediocrity; they are constrained to be robbers....It is said in the towns, 'The Beduwy's mind is in his eyes.' Negligent and impatient, they judge, as they are passionately persuaded, in the seeing of the moment, and then revert to their slumbering indolence." Even the Quran has little praise for them: "The wandering Arabs are more hard in disbelief and hypocrisy, and more likely to be ignorant of the limits which Allah hath revealed unto his messenger." (Sura IX, verse 97)

The bedouin's wild ways have been tamed in recent years by the pickup truck and the VCR. The desert no longer can sustain ever-multiplying tribes like the Awlad Ali, goat-herders and fig-farmers on the north-west coast. Their once-pristine wandering grounds have been crisscrossed by four-lane highways and four-wheel-drive tracks, and punctuated with signboards, rest stops, oil rigs, quarries and factories. In the Eastern Desert a recent drought has reduced the livelihood of the nomadic Bisharin, a tribe whose matted hair, grass skirts and bare-breasted women used to shock the people of the valley. Even in the Sinai Peninsula, a last bastion of nomadic life, the exigencies of getting by have pressed many into permanent villages and jobs in tourism. Their elaborate codes of tribal law are being replaced by courtroom litigation and police control.

Oasis life has changed, too. Paved roads and bus routes tie even Farafra, the smallest and most remote desert settlement, to Cairo. Farmers on donkeyback still splash through the canals that water the rich orchards of Bawiti in the Bahariya Oasis, but they return home to catch the evening's Hollywood soap opera and dine on Danish cheese. The language of Siwa, related to Berber dialects spoken further west, is giving way to the Arabic of the television and schoolroom.

For Westerners the romance of such desert epics as *Lawrence of Arabia* is long vanished. In its place has come a new accessibility and a new kind of traveler. Archeologists, oilmen and northern European housewives now tread where only tribesmen and explorers once ventured. The hot springs of Bahariya and Dakhla, where one can sit steaming under starlight filtered through palm fronds, have been targeted for development as health spas. Planeloads of tourists now fly directly into Sinai, where scheduled camel treks patrol the scenic sites of the interior: the fertile wadis of Feiran and Ain al Furtaga, the pharaonic remains at Serabit al Khadim and Wadi Maghara, the canyon of Wadi Garandal.

After fifteen centuries of splendid seclusion, the Greek Orthodox monks at Saint Catherine's Monastery now endure a perpetual stream of camera-toting visitors. Below the monastery and its priceless collection of manuscripts, its exquisite mosaics and icons, its treasures given by the Russian Czars, hum the engines of squadrons of tour buses. Cairo's ministries even have plans to run a telpher up Mount Sinai. One day perhaps ministers will step from their Mercedes and be whisked effortlessly to the spot where Moses met his maker. Yet all the excesses of the tourism industry cannot detract from the desert's natural splendor. After all, there is no shortage of room for roaming around.

The Egyptian desert may appear forbidding, but anyone who comes to know its many and varied aspects can never be free of its allure. At midday it seems bland and empty of color. But in the softer light of dusk (or of a decent brown-tinted pair of sunglasses) subtle shades emerge. A touch of imagination brings forth the drama: crimson cliffs streaked with black, whipped-cream hummocks mushrooming abruptly out of grey sand plains, walls of peppermint rock, salmon-gold dunes so soft as to be erotic.

The Monastery of Saint Catherine, founded by the Emperor Justinian in the sixth century A.D., is inhabited by Greek Orthodox monks. This remote outpost of Christianity contains a rich collection of artworks, including Byzantine mosaics, icons and manuscripts.

We have all heard about mirages, but nothing prepares you for the desert's games. The very openness of the land plays trompe l'oeil tricks of scale. Little humps look like giant mountains. Spiky ranges seem to be mere hillocks. Scattered on the ground, ten-million-year-old seashells and million-year-old forests of petrified wood testify to the land's experience of richer times. The rocks themselves – fingers of crystallized iron, translucent orbs of red and gold, disks which when cracked open reveal new worlds – seem to speak.

And of course there is the silence, the best cure for this age of haste and noise. No other place on Earth can feel so free of time and space.

The high plateau surrounding Saint Catherine's Monastery has a harsh, unworldly beauty. This forbidding land is the wilderness in which the fleeing Hebrews, led by Moses, are said to have wandered for forty years. Despite the remoteness, flat wadis make for easy access by four-wheel-drive vehicles or camels.

Giant natural sphinx's paws lend weight to the theory that Ancient Egyptians drew artistic inspiration from the desert landscape. The soft sand here, near the Pyramids of Giza, is speckled by hoofprints. A number of stables rent sturdy Arabians by the hour. The open desert, just minutes away from crowded Cairo, is ideal for riding.

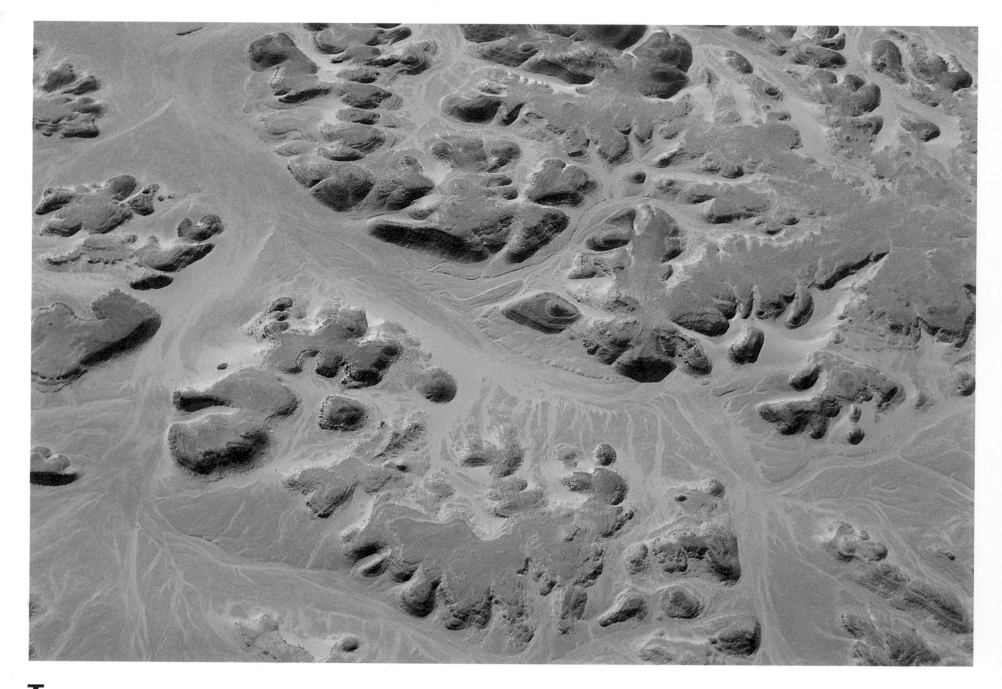

The imagination can easily conjure up fiery patterns from the barrenness near Aswan. The desert is just as fascinating up close, where the extraordinary effects of wind erosion, crystallization and fossilization can be seen. Much of the Egyptian desert was once under water, and it is not unusual to find snail-shells and shark's teeth hundreds of kilometers inland.

The sense of scale is completely lost here, but not the sense of the grandeur and forbidding nature of the desert. Near Aswan it rains very seldom, not more than half a dozen times a year. Yet the rain – along with wind – carved out this unusual topography over millions of years.

FOLLOWING PAGES: The abandoned Monastery of Saint Simeon near Aswan once housed 300 monks. Built in the sixth century A.D., it is a splendid example of sophistication in mudbrick architecture. It was abandoned in the Middle Ages after successive bedouin raids.

These beasts have just completed the Darb al Arbaeen – the ancient caravan Track of Forty Days that brings them from western Sudan to the great camel market at Deraw near Aswan, where they are sold. Most are then shipped to the secondary market in Cairo, and end their days in the city's slaughterhouses – a sad fate for such noble animals.

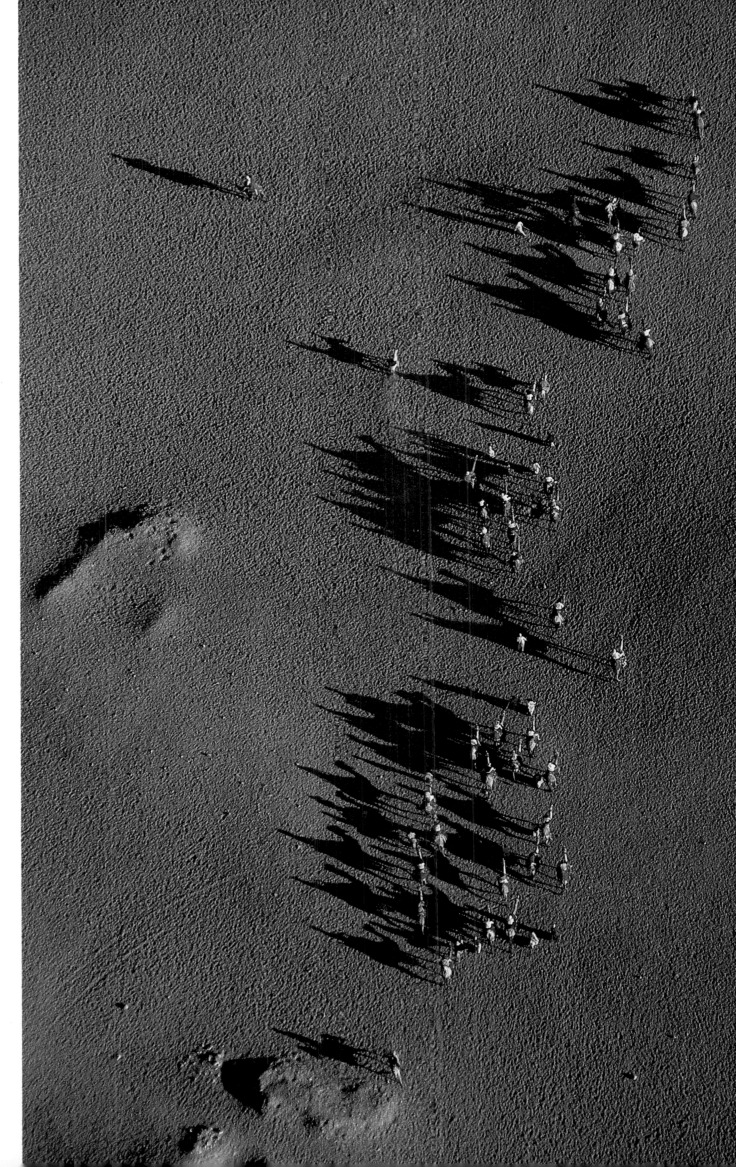

Tourists, with their minders, make up another sort of caravan – on the ritual desert camel ride. Turn the photograph sideways: Elongated shadows evoke one of the camel trains of the past – pilgrims to Mecca or traders of spices, salt, slaves and gold. Sadly, trans-Saharan trade has almost vanished.

FOLLOWING PAGES: Sediment washed out of these spiky mountains has created a wide beach on the western coast of Sinai. Judging by the tire tracks, it has rained since the last vehicle passed.

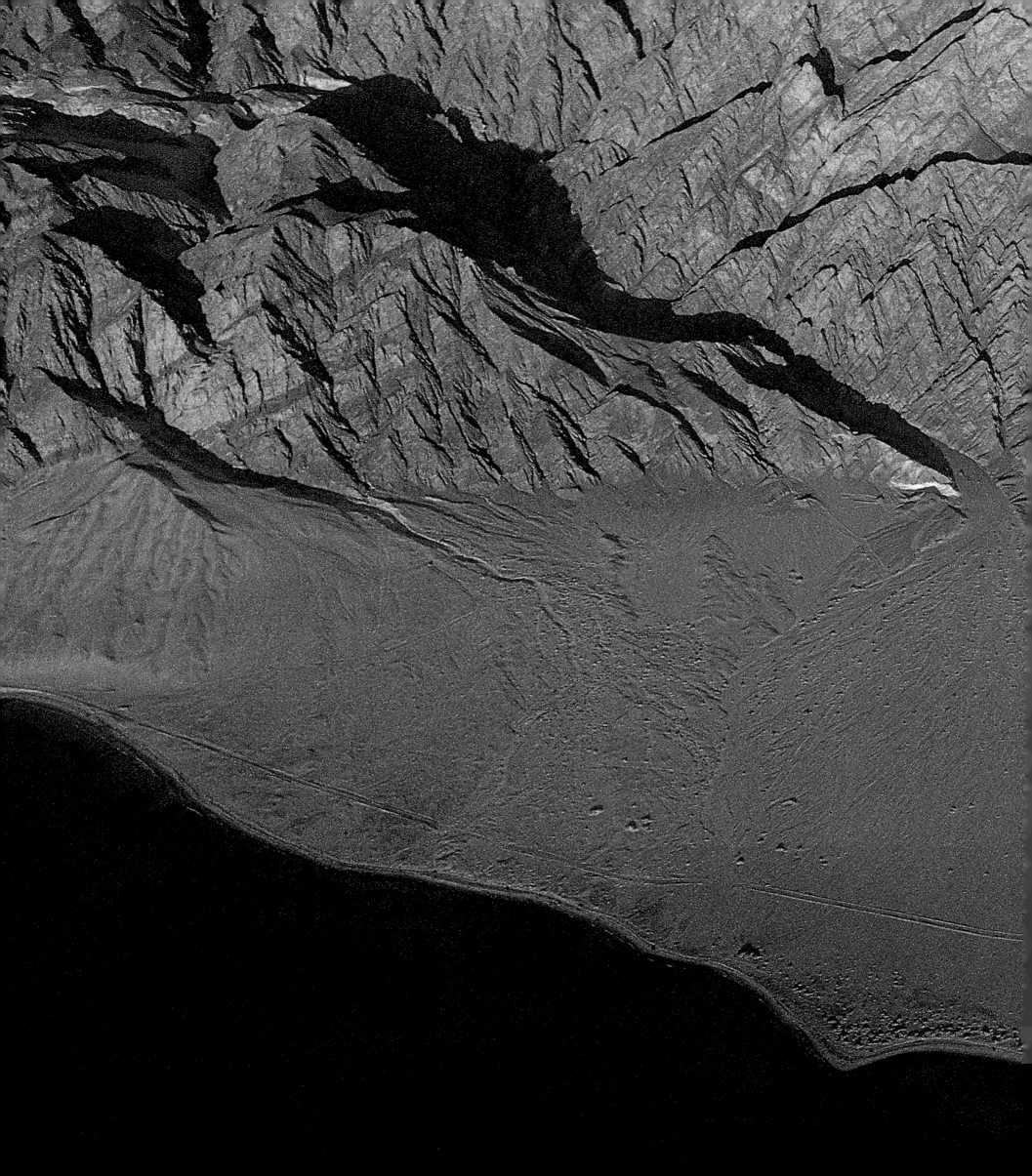

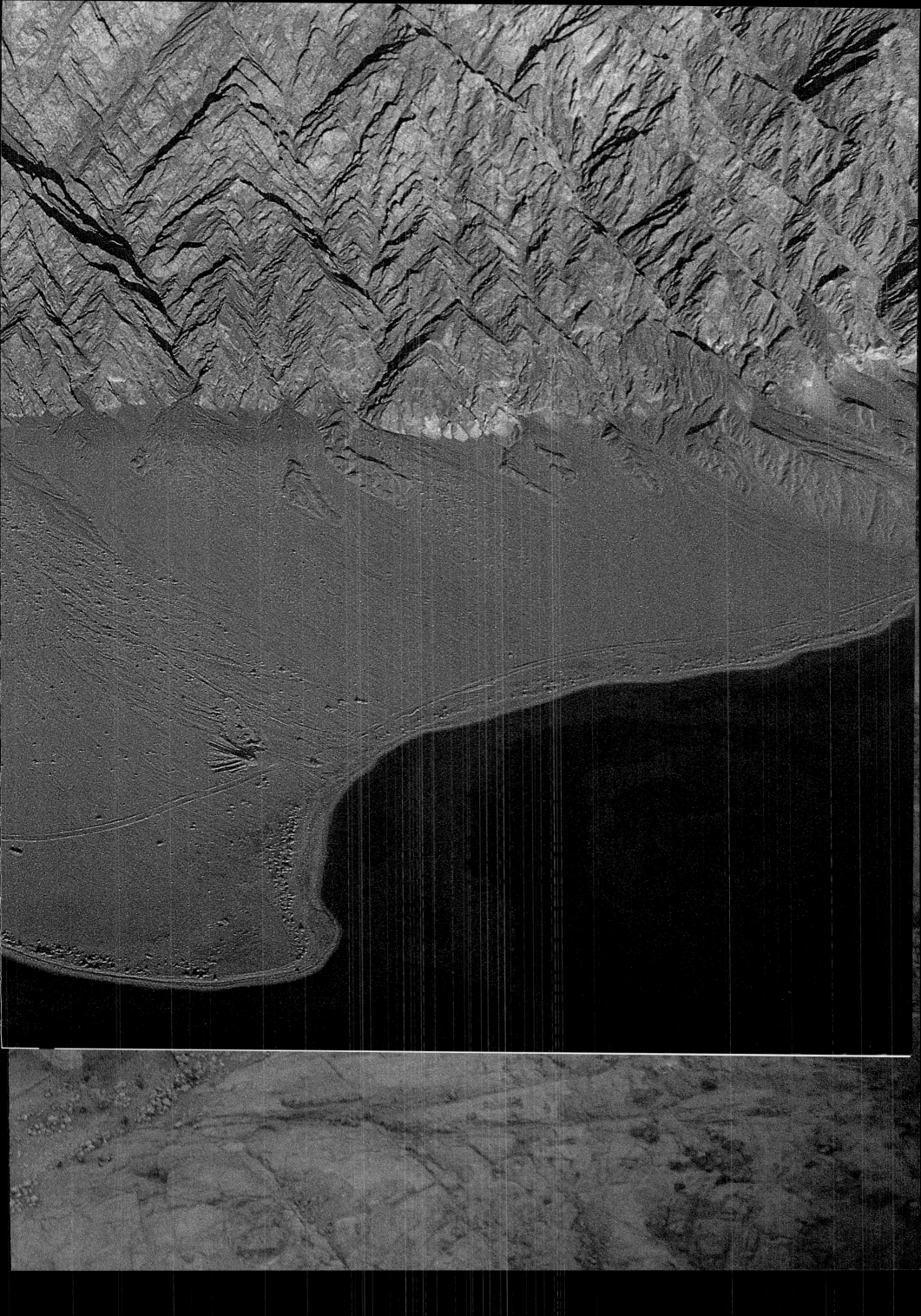

Planted deep

THE SEA

The Ancient Egyptians were not a seafaring people. Their Red Sea shore was dry and separated from the Nile by several days' perilous travel. Their Mediterranean coast lacked a natural harbor. Unlike the wandering Phoenicians they had no cedar forest to plunder for shipbuilding. Unlike the Greeks their land was not so poor as to drive them abroad in search of fortune. It wasn't until late in ancient times that Egyptians turned their attention seawards. Necho, one of the last great Pharaohs, sent a team to circumnavigate Africa in the seventh century. Departing from the Red Sea it returned months later from the Mediterranean, bringing strange tales of the Land of Punt and beyond. Necho even planned to dig a canal to link the Nile to the Red Sea, but the idea was dropped when an oracle advised that such an endeavor would work to the benefit of "barbarian" foreigners. Few prophecies have been so acute. In fact, the first canal was completed by the invading Persians in the following century. It remained in use for much of the next thousand years, until Egypt's Arab rulers, fearing that Byzantine pirates might use it to mount an attack on the holy city of Mecca, allowed it to silt up.

Centuries later the ambitions of a new invader revived the idea. Napoleon dreamed of an even-better canal running from north to south to join the Mediterranean directly to the Red Sea. (The Persians' effort ran east-west from the Nile.) His waterway would threaten Britain's possessions in India and turn the Mediterranean into a French lake. But his engineers abandoned the project after they calculated – wrongly – that the Red Sea was thirty meters higher than its northern sister. They thought a canal would simply drain one body of water into the other.

It took fifty more years for another ambitious Frenchman, Ferdinand de Lesseps, to find both the money and a willing Egyptian patron for his Suez Canal project. Completed in 1869, it radically increased Egypt's strategic importance in the eyes of competing European powers. But as the pharaonic oracle had predicted, Egypt was to receive little reward. The British government managed to buy up the heavily indebted Egyptians' share for a pittance. Soon a British army would be manning the waterway. It was not to be completely dislodged until the Suez War of 1956. As an editorial contemporary with the canal's opening noted, the waterway had been "cut by French energy and Egyptian money for British advantage."

But let us return to the past. The lack of a Mediterranean port was a problem addressed by Egypt's first European ruler, Alexander the Great. Noting the favorable site of the Island of Pharos, he ordered a causeway built to tie it to the shore and form a harbor. The new port prospered, bringing Egypt irretrievably into the Mediterranean world.

Under the wise rule of Alexander's heirs, the Ptolemies, Alexandria achieved preeminence in the Mediterranean. Royally patronized academies like the famous Mouseion and library attracted the best minds of the

Pharaonic temples inspired the high columns and austere façade of Alexandria University's Faculty of Architecture.
PRECEDING PAGES: Fishermen haul in their catch on the Mediterranean coast.

Ramleh Station in central Alexandria is the terminus of a suburban tramline. At the left is the Corniche running along the Eastern Harbor. In the upper left is the building site for a new library to replace the famous ancient institution that vanished 2,000 years ago. The royal palace of the Ptolemies, who made Alexandria their capital, is believed to have stood in the same spot.

Sidi Abul Abbas is the most famous of Alexandria's mosques, although it was designed by an Italian architect in the 1940s. A recent increase in religious fervor made necessary the building of an open plaza for mass prayers. Once the most permissive city in Egypt, Alexandria has grown to become one of the most conservative.

Modern Alexandria sits directly atop its ancient forebear. This small Roman amphitheater is one of the few sites to have been excavated. Among those still to be found are Alexander the Great's tomb, the Library and Cleopatra's palaces.

Hellenic world. The cosmopolitan city's mathematicians elaborated modern geometry, its astronomers conjectured the solar system, its physicians set the bounds of medical knowledge for a thousand years, its scholars translated the Hebrew Scriptures, its poets entertained the known world.

The last ruler of the dynasty embodied the elegance of the Ptolemaic capital. Plutarch describes how the Roman General Mark Antony was seduced by Alexandrine charm: "She came sailing up the river Cydnus in a barge with a poop of gold, its purple sails billowing in the wind, while her rowers caressed the water with oars of silver which dipped in time to the music of the flute, accompanied by pipes and lutes. Cleopatra herself reclined beneath a canopy of cloth of gold, dressed in the character of Venus, as we see her in paintings, while on either side to complete the picture stood boys costumed as cupids, who cooled her with their fans. Instead of a crew the barge was lined with the most beautiful of her waiting-women attired as Nereids and Graces, some at the rudders, others at the tackle of the sails."

Cleopatra so captivated Mark Antony that he betrayed his faithful Roman wife, Fulvia, and abandoned his army to the advancing Parthians to return with her to Alexandria. Yet the Egyptian queen's beauty, says Plutarch, "was not of that incomparable kind which instantly captivates the beholder. But the charm of her presence was irresistible....It was a delight merely to hear the sound of her voice, with which, like an instrument of many strings, she could pass from one language to another, so that in her interviews with barbarians she seldom required an interpreter."

With Cleopatra's suicide and the advance of Caesar's army (which incidentally torched most of the famous library) Alexandria exited its golden age. During the later Roman Empire the polyglot city was torn apart by religious strife. Under Islam's land-based dominion its importance faded. Alexandria's symbol, the famous Pharos or lighthouse, collapsed into the sea. Only in the past hundred years or so, as the Mediterranean again grew in importance to Egypt, has the port city revived. Indeed, earlier in this century Alexandria, with, as Lawrence Durrell said, its "five races, five languages, a dozen creeds...but more than five sexes," gained fashion as an inspiration for writers. Italianate architecture, a thriving stock exchange and a commercial aristocracy with European tastes combined to make Alexandria a Levantine dream city.

But the playground of Durrell and C.P. Cavafy, like that of Callimachus and Theocritus 2,000 years before them, has all but vanished. The cosmopolitan society of the '20s and '30s woke up one day to find itself wholly Egyptian, as if the ancient native suburb of Rhakotis had swallowed up the Hellenic showpiece of the Ptolemies. Just as Alexandria's ancient glories lie buried beneath the modern port of six million inhabitants, its luxurious villas and parks from the early twentieth century largely have given way to tower

The very smell of the sea seems to rise from this boatyard near Alexandria: salt, fresh paint, sodden ropes, fish, diesel fuel. Some of the wooden fishing boats built in Alexandria are ocean-going. The different-sized craft here look like beached tropical fish. Some have been scavenged down to their skeletons.

blocks and factories. What remains of the Alexandrian heyday are the names of its quarters: Glymenopoulo, San Stefano, Miami, Sporting.

Under the pressure of a growing population and of demand for beach accommodation, the city has spread outwards along the shore. Where a generation ago only bedouin goatherds strayed, tourist villages have mushroomed. Egypt's north-west coast – fine white sand and brilliant turquoise sea all the way to the Libyan border – is in the painful throes of a Florida-style development boom.

East of Alexandria, where the Nile's fingertips meet the Mediterranean, change is also the rule. The marshy lakes of Maryut, Edku, Manzala and Burulus, once winter resorts for European wildfowl, are increasingly polluted and empty of fish. Slender fishing punts by the hundred lie idle in the lakeside villages. At the Rosetta and Damietta mouths of the river, massive concrete dikes mar the shoreline. Without them the rising sea-level caused by global warming could submerge much of the Delta. Already the streets of Ras al Bar, a popular holiday town, turn into bathing places where they disappear into the water. Waves lap in beach-house living rooms. Lighthouses built to mark the shore have long been abandoned to the sea. Further east again, beyond the duty-free bustle of Port Said at the head of the Suez Canal, lies the as-yet-undeveloped northern shore of Sinai. As one approaches the tense border with the Gaza Strip, first date palms, then olives and oranges sprout amid dunes as desert gives way to the fertile Palestine plain.

Egyptians call the Mediterranean the White Sea. While it is domesticated and predictable – Alexandria's winter storms, named and numbered, fall on nearly the same days each year – Egypt's other sea is relatively untamed. (Perhaps this is why it is called "red," for there is no other explanation.) Where the Mediterranean coast is mostly featureless sand, the Egyptian Red Sea has a striking, barren beauty. It is lined by spiky mountains, speckled with islands and teeming with fish.

Despite its inaccessibility, the Red Sea was long ago traversed and explored. The ports of Quseir, Berenice and Aidhab served ancient trade routes from the Nile Valley to Yemen, the Horn of Africa and beyond. The Ptolemies imported live elephants, ivory, rhinoceros horn, frankincense, myrrh and of course slaves. They exported, said a merchant of the third century B.C., "undressed cloth made in Egypt for the barbarians; robes from Arsinoë (Suez); cloaks of poor quality dyed in colors; double-fringed linen mantles; many articles of flint and glass…copper, used for cooking utensils and cut up for bracelets and anklets for the women; iron which is made into spears used in their wars against the elephants and other wild beasts…."

Three centuries later Strabo wrote of the growth in Red Sea traffic that followed discovery of trade winds to India: "In earlier times not so many as twenty vessels would dare to traverse the sea far enough to get a peep outside the straits (of Bab al Mandeb). But at the present time even large fleets are dispatched as far as India and the extremities of Ethiopia, from which the most valuable cargoes are brought to Egypt." Pirates abounded and merchant vessels carried teams of archers to defend their Indian treasures of gemstones, silks and spices.

In medieval times the Red Sea ports served the pilgrimage to Mecca, enjoying particular prosperity when the marauding Crusaders made land-passage through Sinai dangerous. Arab dhows sailed all the way to China. Coffee from the Yemeni port of Mocha was landed at Quseir, trekked through the desert on camelback to the Nile Valley and floated down to Cairo. With the coming of steamships and the extension first of the railway and then the canal to Suez, the smaller Red Sea ports declined almost to the point of extinction. Until the 1950s all 1,200 kilometers of coastline from Taba on the Israeli border to Ras Banas far down the Red Sea were practically uninhabited. Since then two sources of wealth have been discovered that should assure prosperity into the future: oil and tourism.

One of the two inlets that frame the Sinai Peninsula, the shallow Gulf of Suez, is striped with pipelines and dotted with oil rigs whose burn-off flares glow offshore in the night. Near the oil-refining port of Suez freighters, tankers, liners and warships mingle as they wait for the next northbound canal convoy.

The thousand-fathom-deep Gulf of Aqaba, on the other hand, is home to beach hotels and a new breed of fanatics: scuba divers. In dramatic contrast to the scorched and empty desert shore, the sea a few steps away erupts with a carnival-like abundance of life. The variety of colors, shapes and habits among the sea creatures is astounding; first-time visitors to the watery jungle often emerge speechless. Two thousand species of coral live here in the massive condominiums they share with untold numbers of fish. Sharks, barracuda and other fierce predators abound, as well as more timid schools of coralfish, angelfish, parrotfish and the like. The African coast of the Red Sea has a similar abundance of marine life, but its shore is less dramatic. The best diving and fishing is to be found off desert islands like Giftun and Shadwan.

Organized tourism has only just discovered the Red Sea – but it has caught on in a big way. Resorts like Hurghada, Safaga, Sharm al Sheikh and Nuweiba have a boom-town atmosphere, with rows of Post-Modern and Moorish-style luxury hotels

Yachts drop scuba divers at Ras Muhammad, a nature preserve at the southern tip of Sinai. The coral reef here is said to be richer in marine life than any other in the world.

lining the beaches. Most of the surrounding coast remains blessedly unspoiled, except for the occasional oil spill.

In recent years Cairo's bureaucrats have increasingly recognized the need to protect the Red Sea's delicate environment. Ships that pollute are now fined. A wildlife sanctuary has been created at Ras Muhammad on the southern tip of the Sinai. One can only hope that Egypt will learn from mistakes made elsewhere, and preserve the Red Sea's pristine beauty from the greed of developers.

Egypt's Red Sea coast is, for the most part, pristine and unspoiled. The contrast between the desert shore and the abundance of life in the water — a veritable aquatic jungle — is astonishing. In recent years petroleum and tourism have lured investors here. Empty stretches like this are giving way to tourist villages and oil derricks.

The fifteenth-century Fortress of Sultan Qaytbay, in the background, stands on the site of the ancient lighthouse that was one of the Seven Wonders of the World. Private yachts and fishing boats mingle in Alexandria's Eastern Harbor, just as tin shanties and apartment blocks mix on shore. The city protrudes like a letter T from the coast, with each arm embracing a harbor. The Western Harbor is more commercial.

Alexandria's main railway station typifies the city's Old World look. Alexandria is tidier and greener than Cairo, to which it is joined by hourly rail and bus services. But as in the capital, modern greed has done away with much of the port city's cosmopolitan charm, with highrises usurping gardens and pollution spoiling once-spotless beaches.

Avenue al Horreya, one of Alexandria's major traffic arteries, follows the course of the ancient Canopic Way leading eastward to the mouth of the Nile. Public buildings line the road: schools, hospitals and departments of the University. Because the city stretches thinly along the coast, traffic regularly backs up on east-west roads like this, particularly in the summer beach-going season.

The palm-filled gardens at Montazah, the Egyptian royal family's private seaside estate near Alexandria, have been turned into a public park. Gazelles once roamed the 250 acres of grounds. At right, the bay at Montazah. In the foreground stands the Turco-Florentine-style palace where King Farouk summered until his exile in 1952. The Palestine Hotel to its right, built for a summit meeting of Arab leaders in the 1960s, adds a modern touch. Sadly, much of the park has been sold off to developers. The row of beach chalets just visible behind the palace are reserved for senior government officials.

A fishing village hugs an inlet on the Nile near the river's mouth at Rosetta. In the distance, beyond a sea of palms, is the sea itself. The Mediterranean here is slowly eating away at the coastline, requiring construction of enormous concrete dikes. The river at its final stage is so well tamed that houses are built right up to the low banks. These little trawling vessels feed the Egyptians' passion for seafood. In summer the restaurants and fish markets of Alexandria are aswarm with connoisseurs of shrimp, crab and other Mediterranean delicacies.

Polka-dots of white table-salt emerge from the striking red of evaporation basins near Port Said.

The finished product is stacked in elongated pyramids awaiting transport.

A fishing settlement at Lake Manzala. This marshy salt lake is one of a chain separated by narrow sand bars from the Mediterranean. Together they form the sea's largest wetland sanctuary for migrating birds. Long, flat-bottomed punts are used by local fishermen, whose isolated villages are infamous as refuges for smugglers.

Port Said is
surrounded by water
on three sides, standing
on a spit of land jutting
into the Mediterranean
between Lake Manzala
and the Suez Canal.
Modern arcades in the
center of the city are
inspired by colonial
buildings such as the
one at the right.

The domed headquarters of the Suez Canal Authority is the major landmark of Port Said. This town of half a million inhabitants at the northern end of the waterway is a duty-free zone. Once famous for the entertainment it offered to passing sailors, Port Said is now better known as a shopping destination for bargain-hunting Cairenes.

Pilot tugboats dock next to a mosque at Ismailia. Ships transiting the Suez Canal pass the waterfront parks of this city at the midpoint of the waterway. The Sweet Water Canal from the Nile (right) winds beside its broad, straight, salt-water sister. Opened in 1869, the Suez Canal has since been deepened and widened three times. Now all but the biggest, fully laden supertankers can pass through it. After Israel captured Sinai in 1967, the Suez Canal was thought to be an impenetrable defense. Some of the crossing points where the Egyptian army built pontoon bridges in 1973 can be seen on the opposite bank.

Fishing boats moor at an inlet in the Great Bitter Lake while their owners repair nets on the sandy shore. The Suez Canal cuts through this small inland sea, which has become a popular vacation spot. It lies only an hour's trip through the desert from Cairo.

A huge container vessel surges through the Suez Canal. Three convoys pass every day in alternate directions, lining up at Suez or Port Said to await their turn. The canal is perhaps the most vital strategic waterway in the world. Shipping tolls bring the Egyptian treasury more than a billion dollars a year. Nationalization of the canal in 1956 spurred an invasion of Egypt by France. Britain and Israel.

A man-made beach on the Great Bitter Lake awaits summer crowds. A wave of tourist development has transformed the inland sea, which was long restricted to military use. The shallow lake, with its beautifully clear water, is ideal for swimming.

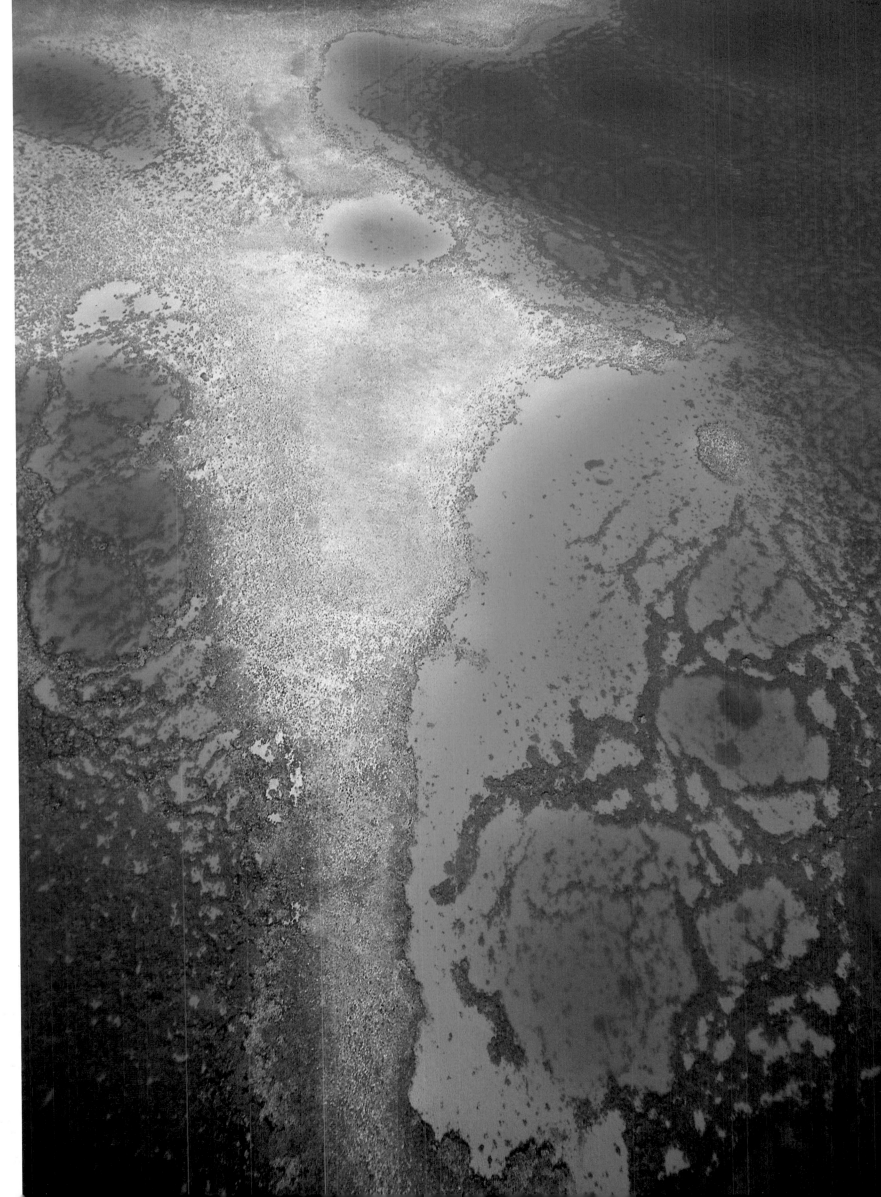

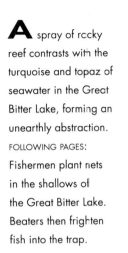 spray of rocky reef contrasts with the turquoise and topaz of seawater in the Great Bitter Lake, forming an unearthly abstraction. FOLLOWING PAGES: Fishermen plant nets in the shallows of the Great Bitter Lake. Beaters then frighten fish into the trap.

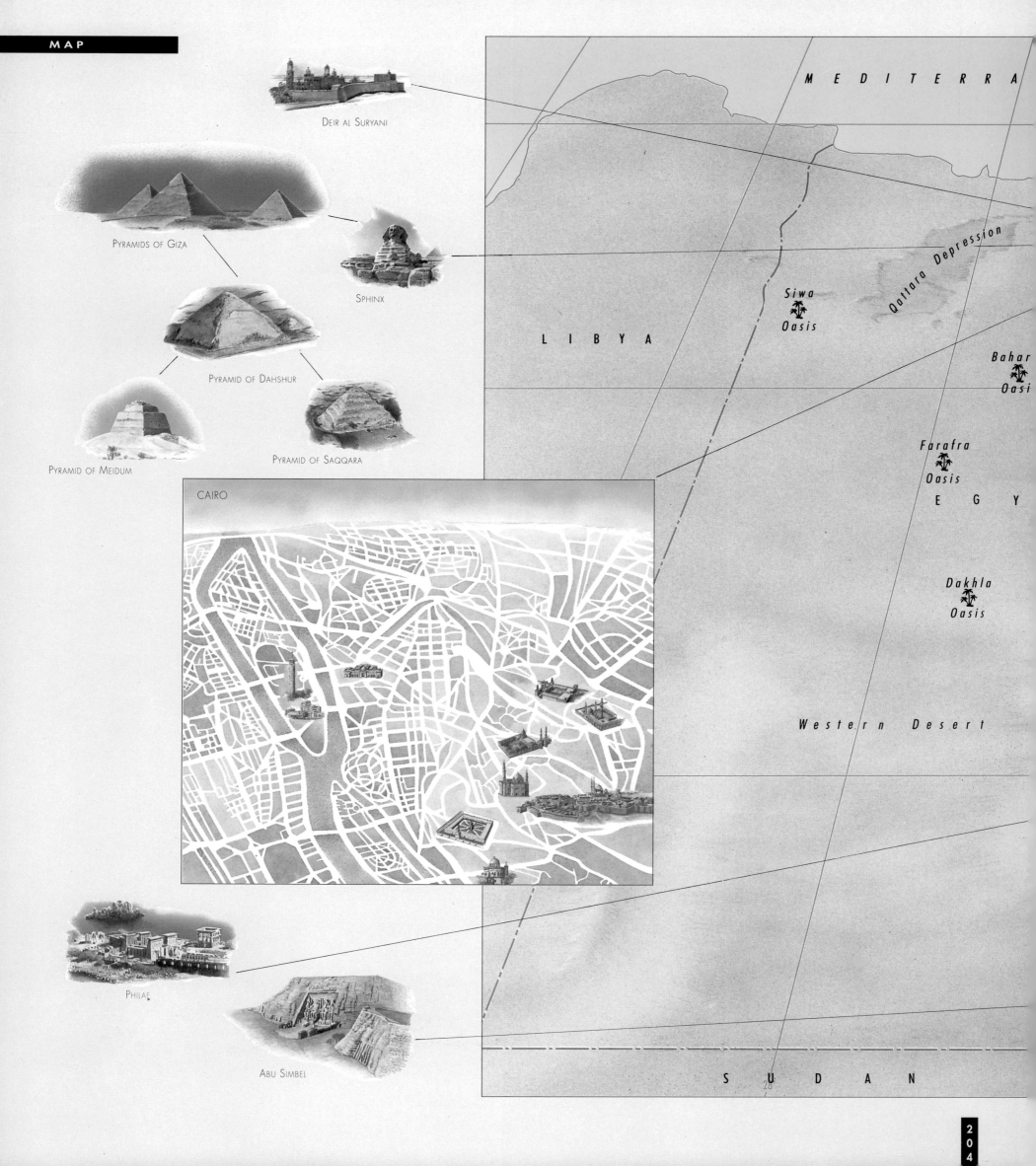

Deir al Suryani

Pyramids of Giza

Sphinx

Pyramid of Dahshur

Pyramid of Meidum

Pyramid of Saqqara

CAIRO

Philae

Abu Simbel

MEDITERRA

LIBYA

Qattara Depression

Siwa
Oasis

Bahar
Oasi

Farafra
Oasis

E G Y

Dakhla
Oasis

Western Desert

S U D A N

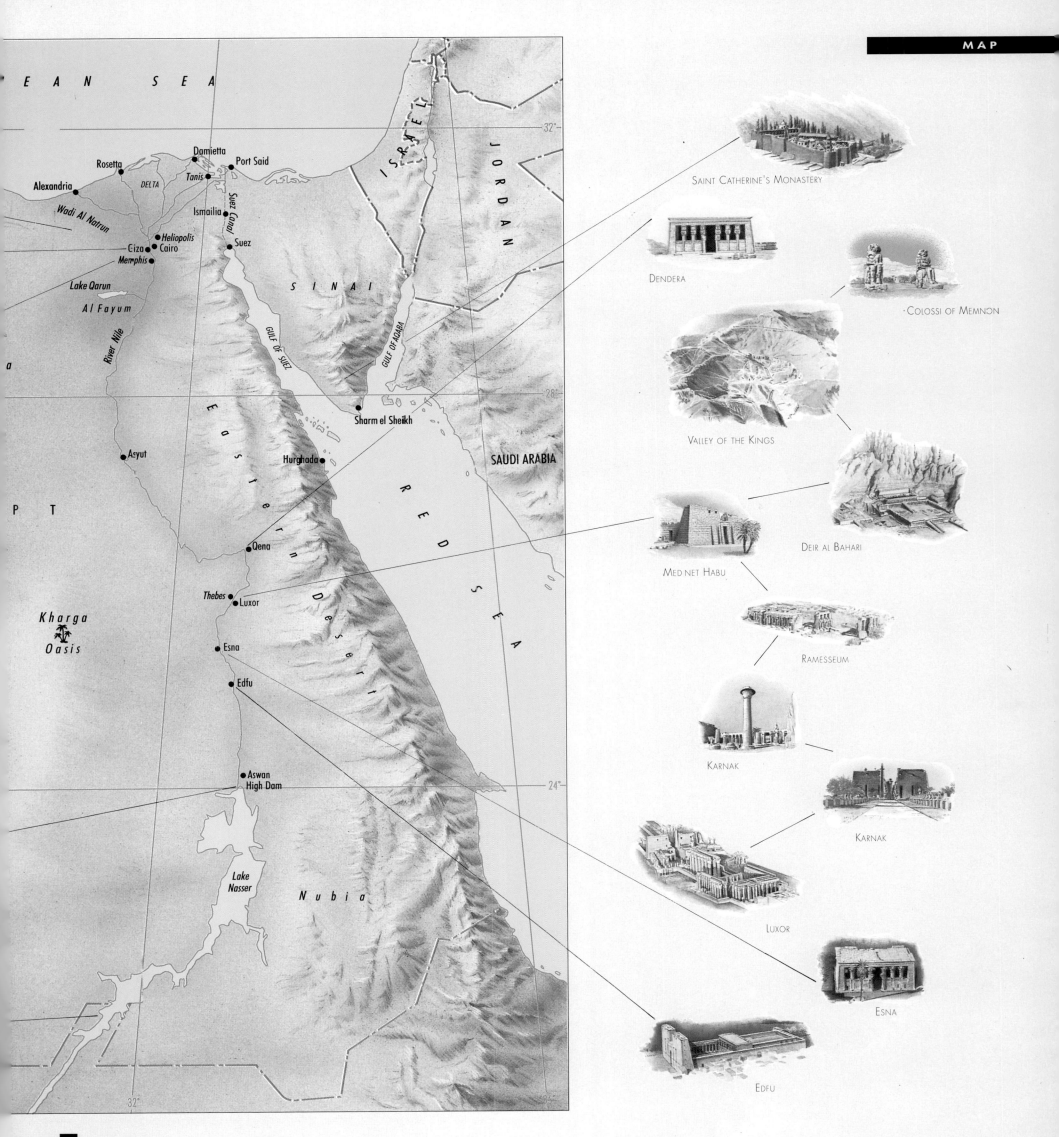

EAN SEA

Damietta
Port Said
Rosetta
Tanis
Alexandria
DELTA
Ismailia
Wadi Al Natrun
Heliopolis
Suez
Giza • Cairo
Memphis
Lake Qarun
Al Fayum
River Nile

ISRAEL
JORDAN

32°

SINAI

GULF OF SUEZ
GULF OF AQABA

Suez Canal

28°

Sharm el Sheikh

SAUDI ARABIA

Asyut

Hurghada

Eastern Desert

RED SEA

Qena

Thebes • Luxor

Kharga
Oasis

Esna

Edfu

Aswan
High Dam

24°

Lake
Nasser

Nubia

32°

Saint Catherine's Monastery

Dendera

Colossi of Memnon

Valley of the Kings

Deir al Bahari

Med net Habu

Ramesseum

Karnak

Karnak

Luxor

Esna

Edfu

A

Abbasid: 70, 73, 86
Abu al Haggag, mosque: 60
Abu Rudeis: 168
Abu Simbel: 20, 23, 24, 35, 66, 112
Abydos: 33
Africa: 21, 106, 123
Aga Khans: 111
Aidhab: 181
Ain al Furtaga: 156
Alamein, Al: 150
Alexander the Great: 35, 60, 155, 176, 179
Alexandria: 19, 22, 23, 35, 70, 76, 150, 176-181, 186, 187, 188, 191
Ali, Muhammad: 75; Palace: 78; Mosque: 92
Amenemhet I: 143
Amenhotep III: 47, 60, 153
American Civil War: 76
Ammon: 153
Amun: 31, 57, 59
Andalusia: 73, 91, 97
Aqaba, Gulf of: 150, 182
Arab League: 76
Arabia: 73, 106
Aramaic: 153
Armenia: 73
Arsinoë: 181
Asi, Amr Ibn al, Mosque: 88
Aswan: 13, 20, 23, 106, 108, 109, 111, 112, 115, 123, 160, 161, 164; High Dam: 13, 36, 65, 106, 123
Avenue al Horreya: 187
Awlad Ali: 155
Azhar, Al: 73, 94

B

Bab al Futuh: 96
Bab al Mandeb: 181
Bab al Nasr: 85
Bab Zuwayla: 84
Baghdad: 36, 86
Baghdadi, Abdul Latif: 75
Bahariya Oasis: 156
Bahr Yusuf: 143
Bawiti: 156
Bedouin: 152, 155, 160, 169, 170, 172, 181
Belzoni: 27

Berber: 156
Berenice: 181
Bisharin: 155
Book of the Dead: 49
Britain: 25, 36, 76, 176

C

Caesar, Julius: 47, 179
Caesarion: 47
Cairo: 13, 16, 21, 22, 25, 35, 36, 40, 70-103, 106, 107, 111, 112, 133, 154, 156, 159, 182, 186, 198
Callimachus: 179
Canopic Way: 187
Cape of Good Hope: 75
Cavafy, C.P.: 179
Champollion: 33
Cheops: 30, 32, 40, 44
Chephren: 30, 32, 40
China: 70, 182
Christianity: 16, 30, 35, 36, 155, 172
Citadel: 13, 22, 25, 70, 78, 89, 92
City of the Dead: 76
Cleopatra: 47, 179; needles: 18
Colossi of Memnon: 48
Constantine: 35
Coptic: 70, 75, 76
Corniche: 99
Crusaders: 150, 182
Cydnus: 179

D

Dahshur: 30, 39
Dakhla: 153, 156
Damascus: 36
Damietta: 181
Darb al Arbaeen: 164
Decius: 61
Deir al Bahari: 52
Delta: 33, 70, 106, 112, 135, 137, 144, 145, 181
Dendera: 33, 35, 35, 46, 47, 62
Deraw: 164
Description de l'Egypte: 18
Desert, Eastern: 70, 150, 151, 155 Desert, Sahara: 153
Desert, Western: 30, 45, 154
Doqqi, District: 98

Doughty, Charles: 155
Druze: 96
Durrell, Lawrence: 179
Dynasty, First: 30; Third: 150; Sixth: 30; Twelfth: 108; Eighteenth: 150; Nineteenth: 35

E

Edfu: 27, 33, 35, 62, 111
Edku: 181
Egyptian Museum: 101
Esna: 33, 35, 37, 61, 122
Ethiopia: 106, 111, 181
Europe: 16, 18, 33, 36, 73, 75, 179; Europe, Middle: 76

F

Farafra: 156
Farouk, King: 71, 76, 188
Fatimid: 73, 75, 84, 96
Fayum, Al: 35, 45, 106, 107, 108, 140, 143, 154
Feiran, wadi: 156
Flaubert: 18
French: 18, 75, 76,176
Fulvia: 179

G

Gabal, Al: 108, 137
Gaza Strip: 181
Gezira Club: 100
Gezirat Faraon: 150
Giftun: 182
Giza (pyramids): 16, 22, 23, 30, 32, 33, 35, 40, 41, 44, 70, 82, 150, 159
Ghuri, Sultan al: 91
Glymenopoulo: 181
Gnostics: 155
Golden Mile: 99
Great Bitter Lake: 198, 200, 201
Greek: 16, 30, 35, 70, 76, 106, 108, 153, 176; Orthodox: 156
Gulf of Aqaba: 150, 182
Gurna: 126

H

Hassan, Sultan, madrasa: 25, 71, 90
Hakim, Al, Mosque: 85, 96
Hathor: 46, 47, 62

Hatshepsut: 52, 57
Hebrew: 16, 157
Heliopolis: 33, 35
Hellenic: 179
Herodotus: 16, 21, 35, 106, 153
High Dam: 20, 36, 65, 106, 112, 115, 118; Lake: 112, 123
Hittites: 35
Hollywood: 18, 156
Horeau, Hector: 23
Horn of Africa: 181
Horus: 62
Hurghada: 182
Hussein, Mosque: 94

I

Ibn Khaldun: 75
Ibn Tulun, Ahmed: 70; Mosque: 86
Ilgay al Yusufi, Mosque: 89
Illahun: 45
Imbaba: 72
Imhotep: 43
India: 97, 176, 181
Indies: 75
Isis: 65; Temple: 13
Islam: 21, 30, 36, 60, 70, 73, 179; Museum: 97
Island of the Blessed: 153
Ismail: 103
Ismailia: 26, 196
Israel: 36, 182
Istanbul: 18, 75, 92

J

Japan: 76
Joseph: 33
Justinian: 156

K

Kalabsha: 112
Karnak: 26, 27, 30, 31, 33, 35, 57, 58, 59
Kemet: 106
Khan al Khalili, Bazaar: 94
Kharga: 153
Khnum: 61
Khusrau, Nasir-e: 73
Kiosk of Trajan: 65
Kit-Kat, Mosque: 72
Kom Ombo: 33, 35

L

Labyrinth: 35
Lake Burulus: 181
Lake Edku: 181
Lake Manzala: 181, 193, 194
Lake Maryut: 181
Lake Nasser: 20, 115
Lake Qarun: 106, 108, 140, 141, 143
Lake Timsah: 26
Lane, Edward: 18
Lawrence of Arabia: 156
Lebanon: 73, 96
Lesseps, Ferdinand de: 176
Levan: 179
Libya: 150, 153, 181
London: 18
Lower Egypt: 30
Luxor: 30, 33, 34, 35, 36, 48, 49, 51, 52, 59, 60, 109, 112, 124, 126, 128

M

Mahmoudiya Mosque: 91
Mamluk: 19, 73, 75, 77, 89, 91, 143
Mansoura: 111
Mark Antony: 179
Marrakesh: 76
Mecca: 70, 125, 165, 176, 182
Medinet Habu: 36
Medinet Nas: 102
Mediterranean: 18, 21, 70, 106, 112, 144, 153, 176, 181, 191, 193
Meidum: 30, 44
Memphis: 30, 33, 35, 43
Mena: 30
Mentuhotep I: 52
Mesopotamia: 70, 86, 150
Miami: 181
Mocha: 182
Mongol: 73
Montazah: 188
Moses: 153, 155, 156, 157
Mount Sinai: 153, 156, 170
Mouseion: 176
Muayyad, Mosque: 84; hospital: 89
Mugattam Cliffs: 13
Muscat: 76
Museum, Islamic: 97;

Egyptian: 101
Mycerinus: 30, 40

N

Nag Hammadi scrolls: 155
Napoleon: 18, 19, 21, 75, 176
Nasser, Gamal Abdel: 36, 112
Necho: 176
Nefertari: 66
New Kingdom: 44, 49
New York: 18
Nile: 13, 16, 21, 22, 34, 36, 66, 70, 70, 72, 73, 98, 99, 100, 106-146, 153, 176, 181, 187, 191, 196; Valley: 23, 70, 150, 168, 181, 182
Nubia: 20, 23, 36, 112, 115, 123, 153
Nuweiba: 182

O

Old Kingdom: 13, 30, 43
Opera House: 103
Osiris: 150
Ottoman Turks: 75, 80, 91

P

Pahlavi, Reza: 71
Paris: 18, 59
Parthians: 179
Persians: 176
Pharos: 35, 176, 179, 185
Philae: 13, 23, 25, 33, 35, 65, 66, 112
Phoenicians: 176
Piloti, Emmanuel: 75
Plutarch: 179
Port Said: 146, 181, 192, 194, 195, 199
Port Said Street, Cairo: 97
Ptolemies: 13, 35, 61, 176, 177, 179, 181
Punt, Land of: 176
Pyramids: 30, 43, 44, 82

Q

Qahira, Al: 73
Qalaat al Gundi: 150
Qalaun, Sultan: 73
Qaytbay, Sultan: 185
Qena: 128
Quran: 155

Quseir: 181, 182

R

Ra: 33
Ramesseum: 35, 51
Ramses II: 20, 35, 51, 60, 66
Ramses III: 36, 57
Ras al Bar: 181
Ras Banas: 182
Ras Muhammad: 132
Re: 108
Red Sea: 150, 153, 176, 181, 182, 183
Rhakotis: 179
Rifai, Mosque: 71
Roberts, David: 24, 25, 27
Roman: 16, 30, 35, 36, 61, 70, 153, 155, 172, 179
Rome: 18
Rommel: 150
Rosetta: 181, 191; Stone: 33

S

Sadat, Anwar al: 36, 102
Safaga: 182
Saint Anthony's, Monastery: 36
Saint Catherine's, Monastery: 36, 153, 156, 157, 160, 172; Village: 155; Mount: 170
Saint Paul's, Monastery: 36
Saladin: 70, 73, 150; Square: 89,
Salt, Henry: 25
Samarkand: 36
San Stefano: 181
Saqqara: 13, 30, 43, 150
Sarghatmish, Mosque: 86
Sephardim: 76
Serabit al Khadim: 156
Serapis: 35
Seth: 150
Shadwan: 182
Sharm al Sheikh: 182
Shelley, Percy Bysshe: 18
Shiite: 73, 96
Sicily: 73
Sidi Abul Abbas, Mosque: 178
Sinai: 150, 152, 155, 156, 165, 168, 171, 181, 182, 196
Siwa: 153, 156
Sneferu: 39
Soma: 35

Somalia: 52
Sphinx: 18, 22, 26, 41, 57, 112
Sporting: 181
Strabo: 106, 108, 153, 181
Sudan: 153, 164
Suez Canal: 26, 103, 150, 176, 181, 182, 194, 195, 196, 198, 199
Suleiman Pasha, Mosque: 78
Sunni: 94
Syriac: 153

T

Taba: 182
Tahrir Square: 101
Tanis: 33
Thackeray, William Makepeace: 16
Thebes: 23, 150, 153
Theocritus: 179
Thousand and One Nights, The: 18
Tower, Cairo: 98
Tutankhamun: 49, 60, 101
Tutmosis III: 57

U

Unas: 30, 43
UNESCO: 20
Upper Egypt: 30, 33, 36, 111, 118, 120

V

Valley of the Kings: 21, 36, 49, 126, 150; Nobles: 150; Queens: 150
Vatican City: 57
Volney: 75

W

Wadi al Natrun: 36, 153
Wadi Garandal: 156
Wadi Maghara: 156
Willcocks, Sir William: 111

Y

Yemen: 181, 182

Z

Zaghloul, Saad: 36
Zamalek, District: 100
Zoser: 30, 43

LITERATURE

Abdallah, Yahya Taher; THE MOUNTAIN OF GREEN TEA, London 1984
Duff-Gordon, Lucie; LETTERS FROM EGYPT 1862-1869, London 1969
Durrell, Lawrence; THE ALEXANDRIA QUARTET, London/New York 1957
Erman, Adolf; THE LITERATURE OF THE ANCIENT EGYPTIANS, London 1927
Lane, E.W.; THE THOUSAND AND ONE NIGHTS, orig. 1838, reprinted London 1979
Mahfouz, Naguib; PALACE WALK, Cairo 1979; PALACE OF DESIRE, Cairo 1991; MIRAMAR, Cairo 1978; MIDAQ ALLEY, Cairo 1975
Shelley, P.B.; "Ozymandias" from PALGREAVE'S GOLDEN TREASURY OF ENGLISH VERSE, reprinted London 1987
Simpson, Kelly; THE LITERATURE OF ANCIENT EGYPT, New Haven 1973
Steegmuller, Francis (translated and edited); FLAUBERT IN EGYPT, Chicago 1979

HISTORY AND SOCIETY

Aldred, Cyril; THE EGYPTIANS, London/New York 1987
Bowman, Alan; EGYPT AFTER THE PHARAOHS, London 1986
Cooper, Artemis; CAIRO IN THE WAR, London 1989
Doughty, C.M.; TRAVELS IN ARABIA DESERTA, abridged edition, London 1907
Emery, W.B.; ARCHAIC EGYPT, London 1961
Gardiner, Sir Alan; EGYPT OF THE PHARAOHS, Oxford 1961
Greener, Leslie; THE DISCOVERY OF EGYPT, London 1989
Lane, E.W.; MANNERS AND CUSTOMS OF THE MODERN EGYPTIANS, 1836, republished London 1981
Meinardus, Otto; MONKS AND MONASTERIES OF THE EGYPTIAN DESERT, Cairo 1989
Mitchell, Tim; COLONISING EGYPT, Cambridge 1988
Moorhead, Alan; THE WHITE NILE; THE BLUE NILE, London 1976
Rushdy, Rashad; THE LURE OF EGYPT, Cairo 1965 Selincourt, A. de (translated); HERODOTUS, THE HISTORIES, London 1954
Stewart, Desmond; GREAT CAIRO: MOTHER OF THE WORLD, Cairo 1973
Vatikiotis, P.J.; HISTORY OF MODERN EGYPT, London 1991

ART

Baines, J. and Malek, J.; ATLAS OF ANCIENT EGYPT, Oxford 1980
Behrens, Doris; ISLAMIC ARCHITECTURE IN CAIRO, Leiden 1989
Reeves, Nicholas; THE COMPLETE TUTANKHAMUN, Cairo 1990
Sidhom, Michel; NOUVELLE DESCRIPTION DE L'EGYPTE, Paris 1981

GUIDES

Forster, E.M.; ALEXANDRIA - A HISTORY AND A GUIDE, reprinted London 1988
Insight Guides; EGYPT, Singapore 1988
Kamil, Jill; SAKKARA AND MEMPHIS, London 1983
Murnane, William; THE PENGUIN GUIDE TO ANCIENT EGYPT, London/New York 1983
PRACTICAL GUIDE TO CAIRO, Cairo 1979
Seton, V. and Stocks, W. and P.; BLUE GUIDE TO EGYPT, London 1983
West, J.A.; THE TRAVELLER'S KEY TO ANCIENT EGYPT, New York 1988

The editor would like to thank Anthony Sattin and Sylvie Franquet for their invaluable help. The photographer wishes to express his gratitude to Captain Yahia El Agaty; chairman of the National Aviation, General Elewa and Captain Atiff of the Egyptian Air Force, Commander Enzo Bianchini, and Marco Castoldi of Best Tours.

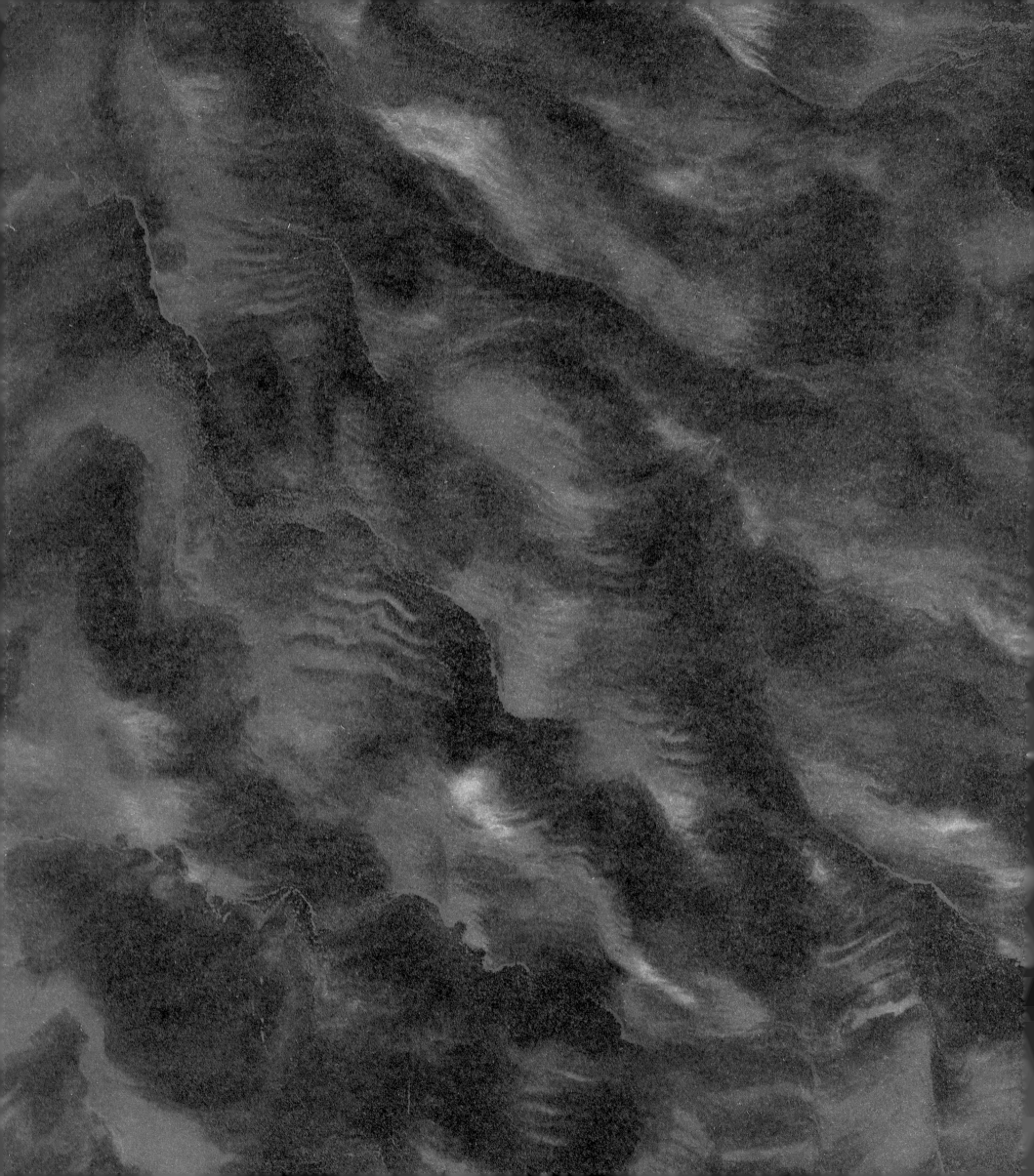